D0418965

THE STATE WE NEED

KEYS TO THE RENAISSANCE OF BRITAIN

MICHAEL MEACHER

Biteback Publishing

To Nigel

First published in Great Britain in 2013 by
Biteback Publishing Ltd
Westminster Tower
3 Albert Embankment
London SE1 7SP
Copyright © Michael Meacher 2013

ISBN 978-1-84954-588-4

10 9 8 7 6 5 4 3 2 1

A CIP catalogue record for this book is available from the British Library.

Set in Adobe Caslon Pro and Knockout

Printed and bound in Great Britain by
CPI Group (UK) Ltd, Croydon CR0 4YY

MIX
Paper from
responsible sources
FSC
www.fsc.org   FSC® C020471

CONTENTS

PART 2: WHY NEO-LIBERAL CAPITALISM MUST BE REPLACED

PART 3: A NEW BUSINESS MODEL: STRATEGY FOR BRITAIN'S RENAISSANCE

PART 4: HOW NATIONAL INTEREST CAPITALISM WOULD RADICALLY TRANSFORM BRITAIN'S SOCIETY AND CULTURE

PART 5: THE WIDER PERSPECTIVE

PART I

UNSUSTAINABILITY: WHAT'S WRONG WITH BRITAIN AND NEEDS FUNDAMENTAL CHANGE

THE STATE WE NEED: KEYS TO THE RENAISSANCE OF BRITAIN

I wrote this book because I was, and am, amazed and appalled at the ideological vacuum which has existed in this country for the last two decades and has neutered politics to the point of banality. None of the fundamentals are even questioned any more; the regime of spin and manipulation has become dominant; and politics at election time has degenerated into a leader personality *X Factor* showbiz contest. Who can remember the defining issues that settled the elections in 2001, 2005 and 2010? Quite – there weren't any.

If the existing system, known as neo-liberal capitalism, was working and fulfilling what most people need – economically, socially, environmentally, spiritually – then all might be well. We could perhaps tolerate the pap which passes for political culture, however shallow and ephemeral, and just get on with our own lives. But it isn't working. It is failing on all four counts. The enduring financial/economic crash speaks for itself. Socially we are becoming a much more immobile and class-bound country. Environmentally the landscape is deeply worrying and becoming (at least at government level) more negative and hostile by the day. And spiritually there is an emptiness and loss of vision endemic throughout the West. Yet hardly anybody says anything;

we need more people like the little boy who observed amid all the cheers about the royal sartorial splendour that the king wasn't actually wearing anything.

So who will speak the truth and tell it as it is? I have never known a time in all my forty years' political experience when there has been such a crying out for political leaders to set out what they actually stand for, yet we are greeted with a resounding silence. Who can honestly tell me any more what is the Conservative, Liberal or Labour line on any of the profound issues that affect our livelihood and society, and what exactly are their distinctly different principles? I think the British people are well aware of all this, but are confused, cynical and angry, and don't know how to get out of what they perceive as a huge political let-down. That is why I have written this book.

The book aims to set out systematically and honestly, in a non-partisan and non-party political manner, what the real fundamental problems facing Britain now are and how they can be resolved in each sphere – in terms of finance, industry, economy, politics, society, environment and our underlying values. It is intended to give a comprehensive picture across the spectrum because all these issues closely interact.

The central issue underpinning them all is the fact, obvious to anyone who looks, that Britain's present course is simply unsustainable. Our economy has been slowly but progressively falling behind our competitors for the whole of the last century. Thatcher did indeed, at a terrible price, greatly improve labour productivity in many key industries, but the market free-for-all which she inaugurated left Britain increasingly unable to pay its way in the world so that the deficit on the UK balance of payments has now reached the unsustainable level of £106 billion a year, 7 per cent of GDP. The reason for that is that manufacturing has been increasingly hollowed out, and finance, which thirty years ago largely covered the deficit in traded goods, even before the crash could cover only half or less.

A second absolutely fundamental problem is the collapse in the level of economic demand. This was temporarily patched over during the last three decades by the colossal build-up in household borrowing (credit cards) and the housing bubble (extracting cash from home equity) to the point where the combined total stood at about £1.5 trillion, larger than Britain's entire GDP. When the bubble burst in 2008–9, house prices fell heavily and households are now subjected to a decade of painful retrenchment. After three bubbles and three bursts in the 1980s, 1990s and 2000s, and faced with the most prolonged stagnation for a century in the Great Recession, where is the demand to drive sustainable growth to come from? This book provides a clear answer to that question.

Another profound problem – and, astonishingly, almost nothing has been done five years on to resolve it – lies in the role, structure and performance of the banks and their relationship with the rest of the economy. The UK banks are over-weighty within an economy the size of Britain's, scandal ridden, poorly managed and not performing their real role, which is to service British industry. The really essential point, which is never discussed, is that the banks focus largely on property (mortgages), overseas speculation, elaborate tax avoidance contrivances and exotic derivatives, and only 8 per cent of their lending goes towards productive and job-creating investment in the UK. This book therefore sets out a radical plan for the restructuring of the banks.

A fourth major issue is the almost universal breakdown in Britain's institutions and power structure. The succession of scandals in banking, political governance, media practices and various aspects of policing has severely undermined the trust and confidence of the British people in the way they are governed. Self-interested individualism has overwhelmed the previous sense of community and personal altruism that bound the nation together and has corrupted the culture and style of the country's institutions too. There is no longer the over-riding sense of communal commitment in the national interest. An unalloyed market system has increasingly caused individuals to look solely to their own interests, leading the most powerful group, the hyper-rich, to establish a degree of inequality unheard of since the Edwardian era. Nor is this just a matter of fairness or social justice, since by pressing down wages and benefits it has disastrously undermined the level of aggregate demand for the economy as a whole.

This book seeks to resolve all these connected questions. It proposes a major revival of manufacturing in high-tech modern form, and explains in detail how this should be done. It sets out how the economy should be rebalanced, notably by regaining public control of the money supply to ensure that a majority of the nation's resources goes into productive investment and job creation on which our future living standards depend. To promote the level of demand to drive growth, it makes the radical proposal of whole-company pay bargaining.

It advocates the break-up of the Big Five banks, which are still too big to fail without colossal taxpayer bail-outs, and proposes a range of smaller banks each specialising in one of the country's needs. It argues that the neo-liberal domination of the interconnected power structure has to be broken in order to make the national interest, not the sectional interest of the rich elite, the prevailing force throughout Britain's institutions. And against the background of deteriorating educational standards, it proposes radical measures to end a class-ridden education system and extend opportunity and aspiration much lower down the social scale, where it is currently lost to the nation.

My qualifications for writing such a book are that I have been an MP for forty-three years, on the front bench for twenty-nine years and a minister for eleven years. But more than that, I have a consuming passion to see Britain revive again and am sickened by the very shallow and partisan level of political debate both in Parliament and in the tabloids, which in my view are so badly failing the country. I am still extremely actively engaged in Parliament – running specific targeted campaigns at the present time on tax avoidance, Atos mistreatment of disabled people in their work capability assessments, blacklisting of industrial workers and reform of parliamentary procedure – and am a constant critic of economic and social policy and of the almost total breakdown in holding the powerful to account. I write a daily blog at www.michaelmeacher.info to pursue these themes and to help organise the campaigns to bring power to those struggling to obtain their rights. Above all I hope that this book may lend inspiration to those who instinctively know that a better world is possible, but who may not yet understand how that can be brought about.

CHAPTER I

A CENTURY OF ECONOMIC DECLINE

(I) THE MEASURE OF BRITAIN'S DECLINE

Britain's century of world supremacy (1815–1914) came to an end at the First World War. By the first decade of the twentieth century its empire spanned a quarter of the world's land mass. Its GDP in 1910 was \$207 billion,[1] almost the largest in Europe and significantly exceeded only by the US. Britain and Germany, with a GDP of \$210 billion, were by far the biggest economies in Europe, with France (GDP \$122 billion) little more than half their size.[2] Only the US, with its vastly larger territory and much higher population, presented much greater economic strength, with a GDP of \$460 billion. In wealth per head of population Britain's dominance was even more marked. Its GDP per capita at \$4,611 was almost half as large again as Germany's or France's or Sweden's, and only slightly below that of the US (\$4,964).

A century later the picture has entirely changed, to Britain's considerable disadvantage. By 2010 Britain's GDP had grown six-fold to \$1.38 trillion, while Germany's economy had grown seven-fold. France, starting from a much lower base, had nevertheless

---

1   In constant 1990 international Geary–Khamis dollars, adjusted for inflation and for differences in the purchasing power of the dollar over time.

2   Maddison, A., *The World Economy: Historical Series*, OECD Development Centre, Paris, 2003; and IMF World Economic Outlook, April 2011.

grown over ten-fold to slightly above the UK level. The US, on the other hand, had far exceeded its European competitors in achieving a twenty-fold expansion of its economy over the previous century to $9.46 trillion. In addition, in terms of GDP per head Britain has again been trailing far behind.

(2) THE CONFLICT OF IDEOLOGIES

What explains this steady century-long relative decline of Britain compared to its main competitors? The period divides into three distinct stages marked by the struggle between very different economic models. Before and after the First World War, the dominant motif was classical macroeconomics (the balanced budgeting of the so-called Ricardian equivalence[3]) until it was finally discredited by the 1930s Depression. Then the new post-Second World War settlement, in repudiation of the deprivations of the previous decade, ushered in the era of managed capitalism and the socialist welfare state, which prevailed for a quarter-century till they too lost their influence amid the hyper-inflation, mainly oil price driven, of the 1970s.

That turbulence paved the way for the third stage, the radical reassertion of market forces by an unleashed neo-liberal capitalism driven by deregulation, privatisation and suppression of trade union power. This stage also enjoyed a quarter-century ascendancy until the long-drawn-out financial crash of 2007–13 demonstrated the explosive dangers of wholly unfettered markets. A fourth stage is now needed which will seek to rebalance the respective roles of state and markets in a more productive and less antagonistic manner, while at the same time addressing both

---

3   The idea that no matter how a government chooses to increase spending, whether by debt or tax, the outcome will be the same and demand will remain unchanged.

the neglected deeper long-term causes of economic uncompetitiveness and social disharmony.

(i) The enforced inter-war austerity

How did each of these stages contribute to the decline? In the first stage the City remained wedded to empire as the prime source of its investments and profits rather than pursuing deeper involvement in and stronger support for domestic industry. Though deeply in debt and dependent on foreign oil to fuel its globally deployed military forces, Britain still issued the world's primary reserve currency. It resolved the problem by setting up the sterling bloc, covering the empire, within which only the pound could be used. Crucially, it forced the biggest imperial creditors, India and Egypt, to keep their net export surplus proceeds in sterling, so that the UK paid for its trade deficit with paper, not real assets. This system prevailed until the US, with a vibrant industry and strong currency pegged to gold, was able after 1945 to offer a sound alternative to sterling for international capital. But throughout the 1920s and 1930s the City preference for high sterling value and priority for overseas deals worked strongly to the disadvantage of British industry, especially after the flawed decision in 1924 to restore sterling to its pre-war rate with the dollar.

The other key strategic failure in the inter-war years lay in macroeconomic errors. The post-war crisis of indebtedness (1919–21) led to the wielding of the 'Geddes axe' in 1922, which imposed budget austerity by massive public expenditure cuts, rather than restoring Treasury coffers by increased tax revenues via an expansionary jobs and growth policy as Lloyd George had promised in his 'homes for heroes' pledge. The result was eight

years of anaemic growth, precipitating the general strike in 1926.
The rigid enforcement of fiscal austerity throughout the '20s
by the authoritarian Montagu Norman, Governor of the Bank of
England, further ensured an unnecessarily long and harsh post-
war recession, paving the way for the stunted recovery, labour
unrest and jobless desolation stretching into the 1930s. A repeat
of the Geddes deflation by the May businessmen's committee,
appointed by the government in 1931, then sharply ratcheted up
unemployment still further, thus lowering tax revenues again, yet
still this prescription failed to restore confidence and achieved
only a partial reduction of the budget deficit. In the face of
two lost decades of the financial authorities' macroeconomic
wrongheadedness, it was only the massive national mobilisation
for the Second World War that finally lifted the country out of
economic stagnation.

(ii) The post-1945 socialist transformation

Following the immense destructiveness of the Second World
War, the political goal in the West was the integration of
economies, to reduce the likelihood of further war, and the
reconstruction of society, to widen rights and opportunities as
an expression of the national solidarity induced by war, as well
as to prevent any recurrence of the penury of the 1930s Great
Depression. The post-war swing of power to the left in favour of
social democracy was reflected in the establishment of a network
of welfare state provisions, a steady diminution over succeeding
decades in the inequality of income in society, the strengthening
of trade union power in opposition to capital, and a widening of
employment opportunities and rights. In particular, faced with
post-war indebtedness amounting to no less than 260 per cent of

GNP in 1945, the Attlee government embarked on a huge house-building and infrastructure programme to absorb the enormous reserves of demobilised labour, rather than pursuing deficit reduction by massive spending cuts as had been tried disastrously twice in the 1920s.

However, by the 1960s, growing pressure from the reviving European economies in higher-value-added products and from developing countries in cheaper staple industrial products exposed Britain's declining competitiveness and lower productivity, requiring tougher measures to improve efficiency. Then, in the early 1970s, worldwide inflation sparked by the quadrupling of oil prices by OPEC necessitated strong counter-inflationary action in all the Western countries. Trade unions, attacked virulently by the Tories and their media allies (*Mail, Sun, Telegraph*), were perceived to have abused their role through the continued and excessive use of strike action, symbolised in particular by the garbage collectors' strike in the winter of discontent, 1978–9. And persistent sniping at the welfare state by the right-wing tabloids on the grounds that it was undermining individual responsibility steadily drained public support from the idea of collective provision against adversity.

While the UK had already slipped back in the international league well before the Second World War, the slide gathered pace after it. Between 1950 and 1980 Britain's GDP doubled while Germany's more than quadrupled, France's more than trebled, and Italy's nearly quintupled. Even the less impressive achievements by the US (trebling) and Sweden (not quite trebling) were far in excess of the UK performance. If anything, the GDP per capita increases were an even bigger warning of how far Britain was falling behind. In Britain the rise was a mere 80 per cent, while in Germany it was 260 per cent, France 190 per cent, and Italy 275 per cent; only the US at 95 per cent had a record similar to the UK, though that was from a high base, whereas the European countries were accelerating away from a low base after the ravages of war. How is this to be explained? One measure for which post-war comparative international data exists is the labour productivity series (i.e. GDP per hour worked). It reveals that between 1950 and 1980 this productivity rating rose 130 per cent in Britain, but at more than double that rate in France and almost three times that rate in Germany and Italy. Only the US did slightly worse than Britain.

(iii) The neo-liberal counter-revolution

The discrediting of Keynesian policies in the 1970s because of excessive international inflation, the loss of confidence in managed capitalism because of trade union disruptiveness in defence of their members' standard of living, the changing perception of the welfare state as a scrounger's charter, as well as the growing awareness that the competitiveness of the British economy was being eroded, all contributed to the sense that a new approach was needed. And once Thatcher was firmly ensconced in power, the gradual encroachment of market forces throughout the 1950s to 1970s within the encompassing framework of social provision was abruptly swept aside in favour of a full-scale unalloyed programme of letting the market rip.

Sharply deflationary monetarist policies, deregulation of finance, privatisation of both industry and services, and the application of market principles to what remained of the economy paved the way for wholesale closures, soaring unemployment, sharply rising inequality and the promotion of business dominance to crush union dissent. At the same time state power was greatly centralised through Thatcher's hegemonic style, and the coercive reach of the police and security services was significantly expanded.

Contrary to all expectations after eighteen years of Thatcher–Major Toryism, these policies were largely continued or even taken further by New Labour after 1997. Deregulation, privatisation and untrammelled market forces remained as dominant as before. The balance of industrial power remained as tilted in favour of big business as it ever was in the 1980s and 1990s, with virtually no changes made to the aggressively anti-trade union laws designed by Thatcher to eradicate union influence. Though some small reductions in child poverty were achieved, the overall inequality in income and wealth remained as wide as in the most extreme Thatcher years, and even wider in the years up to 2005. The centralisation of state power was taken even further, with the country run essentially through Blair's 'sofa government' by No. 10's private negotiations with finance, business and media leaders without checks or balances from either Parliament or the Cabinet. Decisions privately made were then transmitted to the country as a whole via a high level of 'spin' and systematic manipulation of the media.

But did this clean break with the past (though some might see in it a reversion to the classical macroeconomics of the 1920s and 1930s) via a ruthless neo-liberal economic model combined with the politics of hegemonic power jerk the country on to a new higher path of economic prosperity? Clearly in terms of output and productivity it did. During the neo-liberal triple decade of 1980–2010, Britain's GDP rose faster than that of any of the other major European countries. It increased 87 per cent, slightly more than Sweden's 82 per cent and France's 78 per cent, and substantially more than Germany's 51 per cent and Italy's 48 per cent. Only the US, with a 122 per cent rise in GDP, significantly exceeded UK performance. In terms of GDP per capita the UK increase over this thirty-year period was, at 68 per cent, exactly equal with the US and much greater than other main European competitors. In Italy the rise was half that of the UK, in France and Germany it was only two-thirds, and only in Sweden was it near the UK level.

What caused this change in comparative UK economic performance over the last thirty years? Unquestionably there was a very big improvement in UK labour productivity (defined as GDP per hour worked) over the period. It rose by 109 per cent, three times faster than in Italy, and half as fast again as in Sweden (63 per cent) and the US (67 per cent), and comfortably exceeding the rise in France and Germany, both at 81 per cent. That was due to a whole range of factors.

Inflation was reduced, initially through Nigel Lawson's medium-term financial strategy (MTFS), aimed at setting bands for money supply and government debt/GDP, though it quickly failed and was replaced by targeting the exchange rate. The large-scale privatisation of publicly owned assets brought a large tract of industry more directly under the discipline of market forces and through extensive closures raised the levels of productivity and profitability significantly, at least in the early stages – though this did not last. Later balance-of-payments figures show the UK shift from a positive balance of 0.7 per cent of GDP in 1980 to a negative one of –2.5 per cent in 2010, compared with Germany's shift from –1.7 per cent to +5.6 per cent over the same period.

The assault on trade union power by a succession of anti-union legislative Acts dramatically reduced the number of strike days lost through the 1980s and greatly reinforced the capacity of the big corporations to exploit their market power. And the deregulation of financial markets was aimed at consolidating the international competitiveness of the City as a global financial centre, an objective which paved the way for the banking ascendancy of the previous two decades, with ultimately disastrous consequences which discredited the whole neo-liberal and deregulatory model.

There are profound lessons to be drawn from every stage of this century-long pattern of decline. As the inherent unsustainability of neo-liberal capitalism was finally exposed in the financial crash of 2007–8 and the ensuing long recession, the stage is set for a new ideological vision which can draw on those lessons and inspire a different approach, one which combines the imperative of economic competitiveness with the urgent need for social cohesion offering a sense of purpose and identity which has been missing for so long. The rest of this book is designed to set out the blueprint for such an approach.

CHAPTER II

THE FRACTURING OF BRITISH SOCIETY

(I) AN INCREASINGLY IMMOBILE AND RIGID SOCIETY

Social mobility is a measure of the extent of equality of economic and social opportunity, namely the extent to which an individual can make it on their own talents. The increase in upward social mobility which prevailed in Britain throughout the first half of the last century had come to an end by the 1960s. During the period from pre-1900 to 1950–59 the proportion of men who were upwardly mobile rose from 27 per cent to 42 per cent, and similarly for women from 24 per cent to 36 per cent.[4] However, by the 1970s the pattern had begun to reverse. Cohort studies found that poor children born in 1970 had less chance of climbing the social ladder than those born in 1958,[5] and the differences were remarkable. Children with parents in the top one-fifth of earners enjoyed higher incomes in adulthood than those with parents in the bottom one-fifth by a margin of 20 per cent in 1958, but by 1970 that advantage had doubled to 40 per cent. The study placed Britain, along with the US, as one of the least socially mobile societies in the developed world. The US had an

---

4   Heath, A. and Payne, C., 'Social Mobility', in Halsey, A. H. and Webb, J. (eds), *Twentieth-Century British Social Trends*, Palgrave Macmillan, 2000.
5   National Child Development Study 1958 and the Birth Cohort Study 1970.

intergenerational persistence rating (lowest mobility) of .289, with Britain not far behind at .271, while Germany stood at .171, Canada at .143 and Scandinavia between .147 and .139. Measured over time, intergenerational mobility was declining markedly in the UK, even at a time of increasing income, yet there was no such decline in the US.

The reasons for Britain's social stagnation over the last three to four decades are complex, but certainly reflect five key factors. First, the rapid expansion in the first three decades after the Second World War in middle-class professional and managerial positions, particularly in medicine, media, law and teaching, gradually slowed. Children from the lower rungs of the social scale had been able to move up (more 'room at the top') without any corresponding downward mobility from above, but that now came to an end. With the expansion of the middle class halted in recent decades, a middle-class child is now fifteen times more likely to stay middle class than a working-class child is likely to move up into the middle class, while a boy from social class 1 has a more than thirty times greater chance of himself getting a class 1 job (e.g. as a banker or barrister) than a boy from the unskilled working class.

Second, perhaps the most significant social change in modern history, opportunities for women's employment increased dramatically. Professional careers such as medicine, law and management which were previously almost wholly male dominated steadily became equally available to women from middle-class homes, thus squeezing out opportunities previously open to upwardly mobile young men.

Third, the sharp rise in inequality from 1980 onwards meant that those who might before have managed to push themselves upward were now impeded by greater disadvantages.

Fourth, the number of middle-class jobs requiring educational credentials had risen hugely. Of children born in 1958 about 62 per cent left school at sixteen, mostly without qualifications, so that the majority of young adults entered working life on a level playing field, allowing persons without exam success still to reach the top in such varied occupations as banking, policing and journalism. However, once a hierarchy of qualifications began to determine access to jobs at different levels, then, given the close relationship between educational achievement and parental class and income, children from professional homes started with a substantial advantage.

And fifth, a further barrier has been created by the growing need for young people to undergo lengthy postgraduate training and/or periods of unpaid (or very low-paid) internship. Both of these require parental subsidy before young people can enter high-status professions, particularly the law, media and arts.

For these reasons comparative studies reveal[6] that children born to poor families in Britain are less likely to fulfil their potential than in other developed countries. In addition, an LSE study in 2005 found that within Britain itself social mobility had actually declined and young adults were now less likely to break free of their background than in the past. The report also found that only 3 per cent of pupils in the best state schools were entitled to free school meals, compared with a national average of 17 per cent, suggesting that academic selection had been replaced by social selection. Furthermore the study showed that the rapid expansion of higher education during the late 1980s and 1990s had

---

6   Blanden, J., Goodman, A., Gregg, P., and Machin, S., 'Changes in Inter-generational Mobility in Britain', in Corak, M. (ed.), *Generational Income Mobility in North America and Europe*, Cambridge University Press, 2004.

not provided relative benefit to the worst off: quite the reverse. Persons from the poorest fifth of society getting a degree rose from 6 per cent to 9 per cent over the previous two decades, but for the wealthiest fifth it more than doubled from 20 per cent to 47 per cent. This was confirmed further by the Milburn report in 2009, which found that as many as 3,000 students from state schools were missing from the thirteen leading UK universities because their places had been taken by pupils from independent schools with the same A level results, even though the evidence showed that state-schooled pupils performed at the same level as privately educated pupils, even those with higher A level grades, when they reached university.[7]

Even more significantly, further research published in 2007 found that children born in 2000 to the lowest-income households and who scored some of the best results in tests aged three had, by the age of five, fallen behind. By the time they were seven, they had been overtaken by the pupils from the wealthiest homes who had come bottom in the tests aged three.[8] The study concluded that social class is still the biggest predictor of school achievement, the likelihood of getting a degree and even a child's behaviour, suggesting that the advantages of being born in a privileged home have not changed in the last thirty years.

A government report in 2008, however, sought to put a more optimistic spin on the evidence for social mobility when it found that there was a weakening of the relationship between parental income and GCSE achievement at age sixteen for children born in 1990 compared with a cohort born in 1970. But this doesn't necessarily imply any improvement in social mobility at

7   'Unleashing Aspiration', Milburn report, 21 July 2009.
8   Sutton Trust report, December 2007.

all. The most important shift over the last forty years has been the large decline in the proportion of the population engaged in skilled manual work. At the same time the relative earnings of many occupations which require higher levels of education have declined, to the extent that occupations which could be accessed with five O levels in the 1960s now require a degree. The net effect has been that it is now increasingly difficult for children from middle-income households to achieve the relative, and even absolute, living standards of their parents. The harsh reality is that in the bad old days of the eleven-plus there was more social mobility than there is now.

Two studies confirm that the UK's position in the international rankings of social mobility remains very poor. Esping-Andersen found that UK adults have the strongest association between their test scores and their father's education in a study of seven OECD countries. And in a study of fifty-four countries Woessman reported the UK bottom of the international rankings in terms of association between children's test scores and 'books at home' – a proxy for parental income.[9] This matters greatly when economic efficiency depends on making the best use of the talents of everyone, and when social cohesion and inclusion are more likely to be achieved where people believe they can improve the quality of life they and their children enjoy through their abilities, talents and efforts.

(2) THE BALLOONING OF INEQUALITY

Another aspect of the unsustainability of current British society lies in the exponential explosion of inequality over the last three

---

9   'Getting On, Getting Ahead', Cabinet Office Strategy Unit report, November 2008.

decades and its corrosive impacts on the values and cohesiveness of the wider community as a whole. In 1979 Britain was one of the most equal societies in the developed world. By 2010 it had become one of the most unequal – a transformation driven by a huge surge in the numbers and wealth of the mega-rich. Whereas inequality remained largely stable for twenty years throughout the 1960s and 1970s, the Gini co-efficient measure of inequality rose dramatically under Thatcher's neo-liberalism in the 1980s by an unprecedented 41 per cent. Under New Labour it continued to rise slightly by a further 5 per cent.

The ballooning of wealth in such a short period has been staggering. According to the *Sunday Times* Rich List of April 2010, the 1,000 richest multimillionaires in the UK – just 0.003 per cent of the adult population – more than quadrupled their wealth in the eleven years 1997–2008 from £99 billion to £413 billion. Even more remarkably, after slipping back in the 2008–9 crash, they increased their gains again by a further £155 billion in the three years of austerity 2009–12 when almost everyone else in the UK suffered significant real-terms declines in both income and wealth.[10] And according to Tulip Financial Research, specialist wealth consultants, the richest 45,000 people, precisely 0.1 per cent of the adult population, now own one-third of all liquid assets; indeed, the wealthiest 1,000 persons alone (1 in 60,000) now have a total wealth of £1 trillion. This is matched by the trend in incomes. In 2010, according to the *Guardian* Survey of Executive Pay,[11] the average reward for the FTSE 100 chief executive, including bonuses, share options and other incentive schemes, reached £3.75 million (£72,057 per week). This was 145

10   Beresford, P., *Sunday Times* Rich List, May 2012, p. 4.
11   *Guardian*, 16 May 2011.

times greater than the national median full-time wage of £25,800 a year (£495 a week). Nor did this exploding inequality diminish in the post-crash years after 2008. Treasury figures[12] reveal that in 2010/11 the richest 1 per cent of adults in the workforce, that is, 305,000 persons, had an average income of £356,000 a year (£6,850 a week), the even richer 0.1 per cent were paid £1,370,000 (£26,350 a week), while the mega-rich top 3,000 individuals, the highest-earning 0.01 per cent, each get on average an enormous £5,130,000 annually (£98,650 a week). Altogether there are now 619,000 millionaires in Britain today,[13] including nearly 100,000 created by the stock market recovery from the 2008–9 crash as well as by a big influx of rich foreigners.

Two arguments are used to justify this: that wealth creation is more important than wealth distribution, and that wealth at the top harms nobody else. Neither of these stands up to serious scrutiny. Today's runaway executive pay, soaring City fees and record bonuses clearly do not relate to any new entrepreneurial and economic renaissance, since Britain has internationally low innovation and productivity rates. While there are certainly a number of successful entrepreneurs, there is no evidence that today's escalating rewards are linked to historically high and internationally exceptional levels of skill, risk-taking and effort. Rather, the ranks of the rich contain many tycoons, investment bankers and business bankers who have taken advantage of the orgy of speculation, deal-making, financial contrivance and financial raiding in the current wealth glorification culture to swell their own bank accounts at the expense of others. There is very little genuine wealth creation and no trickle-down. Indeed,

---

12   Hansard, 13 October 2010.
13   *Sunday Times*, 20 March 2011.

rewarding failure has become the norm, pay and remuneration have become decoupled from performance ('value skimming', as it has been called), and excessive fee-taking has become routine ('the croupier's take', as it is known in the City). Ineptitude by senior executives (the rewards for which are dubbed 'golden condoms' – they protect the executive and screw the shareholder) has become the shortest route to millionaire status.

Nor is it without harm to the rest of society. A recent cross-national study[14] has demonstrated that inequality isn't just bad for those at the bottom, but for everyone. Analysing data across twenty-one developed market economies as well as the fifty US states, Wilkinson and Pickett found that there are higher prison populations, more murders, more mental illness, more teenage pregnancy, higher obesity rates, greater infant mortality, and less numeracy and literacy in more unequal societies. Their study showed definitively that the more unequal societies are, the greater the social pathology and dysfunctionality across the board. Even the rich report more mental ill health and have lower life expectancies than their peers in less unequal societies. In the most unequal societies mental illness is five times more prevalent than in the most equal, and obesity six times so. Britain's growing social problems are indissolubly linked with the growth of income inequality, which has risen inexorably by some 40 per cent over the last thirty-five years.

During those years in which the richest 10 per cent became more than 100 times as wealthy as the poorest 10 per cent,[15] the

---

14   Wilkinson, R. and Pickett, K., *The Spirit Level: Why Equality Is Better for Everyone*, Allen Lane, 2009.

15   National Equality Panel, 'An Anatomy of Economic Equality in the UK', CASE report no. 60, Government Equalities Office and Centre for Analysis of Social Exclusion, London, 2010.

poor grew hardly better off at all. More than 3.6 million families (about one-seventh) still live below the poverty line, conventionally defined as having an income below 60 per cent of median earnings (i.e. below £230 a week). Nearly one in four adults in Britain is still unable to afford basic necessities such as proper clothing, decent nutrition or repairs to furniture.[16] Of the 12.4 million people – one-fifth of the entire population – living in homes below the poverty line, most, contrary to the conventional wisdom, were not on benefit. Some 3.6 million were children and 2.2 million were pensioners, but 6.7 million were working-age adults. And poverty has become more persistent, deeply embedded and concentrated – half of the children in poverty live in just 6 per cent of the country's 10,000 wards. These deprived communities suffer not only from very low incomes, but also from worse housing, more crime, higher joblessness, more remote health facilities and poorer schools.

Income distribution in Britain remains obstinately onion-shaped. There is a large and scarcely reducing underclass at the base, a majority extended around the national average wage of £440 a week, a growing and prosperous professional, managerial and technocratic class and a tiny group of the mega-rich (less than 1 per cent). This breakdown corresponds quite closely to the power divisions that mark out Britain today – an underclass almost permanently powerless, a majority around the average equipped with basic rights but still often insecurely at the mercy of the economic cycle, a confident and assertive middle class secured by increasing capital wealth, and a plutocracy of the hyper-rich able much of the time to use their immense wealth

16   'Strategies against Poverty', Joseph Rowntree Foundation, December 2004.

and influence to circumvent legal and regulatory controls in pursuit of their power and money ambitions.

Counterposing the burgeoning underclass is this elite globalised super-class, which Rothkopf[17] numbers at around 6,000 worldwide. It is made up of the CEOs of major corporations, partners in hedge funds and private equity, national and religious leaders, a few global political intellectuals, military leaders and some cultural figures. They control oil, money, intellectual property, technology and the media. They go to enormous lengths to keep their activities a private affair, yet their activities are hugely interconnected. A third went to just twenty universities. The directors of the world's top five companies sit on the boards of another 147 major companies. They have ready access to government because of their position, and because they know the politicians personally they can meet annually at Davos via the opulence of their private $45 million Gulfstream jets. They dominate financial power by their almost limitless capacity to borrow cash, leverage it, transfer it across borders, buy up other companies with it and shield it in tax havens. There has not been a gap between the rich and poor on this scale ever in history.

There are several lessons from all this. First, the 'trickle-down' theory isn't working. In fact, poverty levels are affected more by the distribution of income than by total economic growth. Britain has a similar per capita GDP to France and Germany, but the bottom fifth of Britons are 25 per cent worse off than their French and German counterparts because in Britain income is much more unevenly distributed. Second, social mobility is highest in countries with more equal distribution of income

---

17   Rothkopf, D., *Superclass: The Global Power Elite and the World They Are Making*, Farrar, Straus & Giroux, 2008.

and wealth. Sweden's success in equalising life chances through education and childcare strategies has only been possible against a background of reducing economic inequality. Universal child-care coupled with British levels of inequality will not achieve Scandinavian levels of social mobility. Third, several empirical studies have shown that great inequality produces lower levels of trust among citizens and lower levels of political participation. In general, economic inequality is now on a scale that threatens the core values and key objectives of social democracy. Fourth, social mobility has stagnated. Private education as a passport to the top echelons of British society has become increasingly important. While private schools educate only 7 per cent of the total school population, no less than 55 per cent of top journalists, 70 per cent of finance directors, and 45 per cent of top civil servants were privately educated.

(3) EDUCATIONAL PERFORMANCE FALLING BEHIND OTHER COUNTRIES

A major cause both of Britain's growing inequality and of its overall social decline lies in its deteriorating educational output relative to other comparable countries. According to the OECD's Programme for International Student Assessment (PISA), covering sixty-five countries, pupils in Japan, Korea and Finland in 2009 performed well above average in the key subjects of reading, maths and science, while the UK was below average in the first two, though above average in science.[18] Significantly, while Finland and Korea had between 42 and 52 per cent classified as top or strong performers in these subjects and only 6–8 per cent classified as lowest performers, the UK had only 28–34 per cent rated

---

18   OECD, PISA, 2009 database.

as top or strong performers but as many as 15–20 per cent categorised as lowest performers.

Official UK government data, however, appears to provide a more encouraging picture of recent educational improvement among UK pupils.[19] It shows the proportion of pupils achieving level 4 or above at Key Stage 2 rising sharply between 1997 and 2010, from 63 per cent to 81 per cent in English, 62 per cent to 80 per cent in maths, and 69 per cent to 88 per cent in science. Similarly the proportion of examinees who achieved at least two A level or equivalent passes[20] rose from 81 per cent in 1997 to 94 per cent in 2009, while those with three or more such passes rose from 57 per cent in 1997 to 77 per cent in 2004 (later figures are not available).

Nevertheless this rather optimistic impression needs to be treated cautiously for several reasons. First, independent tests conducted by the Curriculum Evaluation and Management Centre at Durham University suggest that GCSE standards may have slipped over the last two decades by nearly two-thirds of a grade and A level standards even more by an average of two grades,[21] so that exam performance may not be improving at all. In addition to grade inflation, there is evidence of savvy schools pushing pupils towards easier, less academic subjects such as sports management or catering. Second, the OECD's PISA assessments of sixty-five countries show the UK has slid down the rankings for international tests. The UK was placed seventh in reading for fifteen-year-olds in 2000, then

---

19   Department of Education, Trends in Education and Skills, 5.3 National Curriculum Key Stage 2.
20   Department of Education, GCENC A/AS and Equivalent Examination Results in England 2009–10.
21   Coe, R., and Tymms, P., 'Summary of Research on Changes in Educational Standards in the UK', in Institute of Directors, *Educational Briefing Book*, August 2008.

seventeenth in 2006, and then down further to twenty-fifth in 2009. In maths the UK was placed eighth in 2000, then twenty-fourth in 2006 (below the average), and finally twenty-eighth in 2009. In science the UK was fourth in 2000, but fourteenth in 2006, and then sixteenth in 2009.[22] The UK was the only country to fall from a top-performing group in 2000 to a lower group just six years later, and then fall further still three years beyond that. This does not necessarily mean that UK pupils' performance has deteriorated, but it certainly does mean that other countries have been improving their performance much faster, and the UK's near-global lead in these three crucial educational areas has been substantially lost in the last decade.

A third factor lies in the polarisation of performance between the private schools at one end of the UK spectrum and the long tail of educational under-achievement at the other – a wider gap than in almost any other country. Among the former, with 7 per cent of UK pupils, 31 per cent achieved three or more grades at A level in 2007, compared with just 10 per cent in the state sector. The private schools provided 14 per cent of the A level candidates that year, but were awarded 28 per cent of the A grades. Similarly for GCSEs, 88 per cent of private school pupils achieved five or more A*–C grades, compared with 60 per cent of state school pupils. In 2010 private school pupils won 4,112 A* grades in maths while the entire comprehensive sector, thirteen times larger in numbers, won only 3,420. In languages the private schools achieved 1,068 A* grades, more than twice the total for comprehensives.[23] At the other end of the range, by

22   OECD (2010) PISA 2009 Results, volume 1, 'What Students Know and Can Do: Student Performance in Reading, Mathematics and Science', figure 1.3.21.

23   *Sunday Times*, 7 August 2011.

international standards very large numbers leave school in the UK without what the OECD calls 'baseline qualifications' (five good GCSEs) – two-fifths of all sixteen-year-olds, fewer than half of whom remedy the failure later. This large, ill-educated group face the second-highest earnings penalty for their lack of qualifications in the OECD, behind only the US, and a high risk of joblessness too.

This divide seems likely to open up further on current trends. Already, according to a recent Sutton Trust study,[24] pupils from private schools are fifty-five times more likely to get a place at Oxbridge than poorer state school pupils; in fact Oxbridge educates more Etonians than boys poor enough to get free school meals. The private schools remain overwhelmingly the gateway to the top professional positions – a third of all MPs, half of appointed peers in the House of Lords, half of the UK's best-known journalists, and 70 per cent of leading barristers. And these schools are now increasingly abandoning GCSEs for the more demanding independent versions aimed at the international market, while despite fees that have doubled in real terms over the last decade the proportion of parents who say they would send their children private if they could afford it has risen to over half.[25] By contrast, at the other end of the spectrum the failure remains stark. In the most deprived areas of England only one in four pupils gains five good GCSEs, one in eight sixteen-to-nineteen-year-olds is a NEET (not in education, employment or training), half the adult population lacks basic numeracy skills and one in six lacks literacy skills. Altogether, despite billions spent on education since 1997, almost 60 per cent of pupils

24 Sutton Trust, 20 December 2010.
25 *Economist*, 4 July 2009.

– 3.9 million over ten years – have left school without gaining five C grades at GCSE, including English and maths, while 1 million teenagers have failed even to achieve five G grades.[26]

(4) THE DEEPENING SOCIAL PATHOLOGY OF AN UNDERCLASS

An inevitable consequence of these widening social and educational divisions is the hardening of a core at the bottom of society, estimated by various sources at around a tenth of the population, who feel alienated, resentful and often hostile because they perceive themselves as marginalised and lacking respect and status in the eyes of others. Joseph Rowntree research findings show that the persistence of poverty from the teens into the forties has risen over time, and the impact of teenage poverty on later outcomes has also intensified compared to earlier decades. But the intergenerational cycle is more multifaceted than the mere durability of poverty and is associated with low parental education, poor neighbourhoods, persisting lack of employment (sometimes through generations) and, for women, single parenthood.

Over the last half-century there has been a profound change in attitudes towards working-class culture. In the 1950s and 1960s the working class was flavour of the times (e.g. in films like *Saturday Night and Sunday Morning*). There was something noble, if harsh, in the condition of the indigenous poor, with angry young men with earthy accents railing against the class structure. Pop culture was transformed by cocky lads from humble backgrounds, and the working class was on its way somewhere, crucially with mobility. But that changed in the

1980s. Those who could get out had left, joining an expanding middle class, and those left behind have become the underclass and stereotyped as feckless, obnoxious and amoral. It has left this sub-class feeling under siege, as if their very sense of self is being called into question. There is an atmosphere of displacement, or impending obsolescence, hanging over such communities, only sharpened by immigration, perceived as a further threat to identity. This profound alienation and perception of being disrespected, coupled with a visceral hostility towards the police, seen as enforcers of a hated social order, became the major triggers of the five days and nights of urban rioting that swept Britain in August 2011.

This demonisation of traditional working-class culture has been coarsened by the Thatcherite shift from community values of solidarity and mutual support in favour of rampant dog-eat-dog individualism. Those who failed to prosper during the boom years are now written off and reviled as a 'chav' rump, a despised sub-culture. The myth of the classless society gained ground precisely as society became more rigged in favour of the middle class.[27] Just as the bankers' doctrine is that the rich simply deserve to be rich, so the poor, white working class deserve to be poor because of the layabout habits of its 'feral' youth.

None of this, however, is to deny that the extent of social breakdown has grown markedly in recent decades. A report last year found that the UK 'poor living environment', based on numbers for teenage pregnancy as well as adolescent drink and drug use, was only worse in Europe in two countries, Estonia and Bulgaria.[28] The proportion of children born out of wedlock

---

27   Jones, O., *Chavs: The Demonization of the Working Class*, Verso, 2011.
28   Relationship Foundation, 2010 report.

has grown five-fold, from 8 per cent in 1970 to 42 per cent in 2004, though that partly reflects the doubling of the number of cohabiting couples over the same period. Binge drinking has sharply increased, with deaths caused by alcohol more than doubling from 4,150 in 1991 to 8,400 in 2005. Another survey has found that British families are the third most pressured in Europe, behind only of those in Romania and Bulgaria, despite UK national income being five times greater. But while many of these indices apply across the social spectrum, the onus for this perceived degrading of British society is firmly placed on its despised underclass.

CHAPTER III

HUMAN SOCIETY: LIVING ON BORROWED TIME

Unsustainability, however, is not only a matter of economic and financial breakdown, combined with a fracturing of social cohesion and communal values, but also a measure of the incompatibility of economy and civilisation with the ecosystem on which human life depends on this planet earth. The present global order is currently despoiling those conditions to a degree that is fast becoming unviable. The key constraints are energy demand, natural resources availability and minerals depletion, all of them exacerbated by exponential population growth.

(I) PEAK OIL AND GAS

The most immediately demanding pressure comes from the impending energy crunch, particularly in oil. The bulk of the world's oil supply derives from organic-rich deposits created in two exceptional periods of extreme global warming, some 150 million and 90 million years ago. Oil extraction began as recently as 1859, in Pennsylvania, but in a mere 150 years half the total global stock of conventional oil, which amounts to about 2.5 trillion barrels, has already been consumed. However, the world is now caught in a pincer between peaking supply and rapidly expanding demand.

On the supply side, fewer and fewer new oilfields are being found. Altogether in over a century only just over 500 giant oilfields (defined as holding more than 500 million barrels, though that is less than a week's global supply) have been discovered. Since 2000, the average size of new oilfields has been just 20 million barrels, below a quarter of a single day's global supply. Already four-fifths of the world's oil supply comes from fields discovered before 1970, and since nearly a quarter of global oil is pumped from the twenty biggest fields in the world and production in several of the top twenty is falling fast, peak oil (the year when global oil production reaches its maximum) is rapidly approaching. Many experts in the oil industry place it within the period 2010–15, though the world economic recession 2007–2013 may postpone it by a few years. If then there is a rapid decline after the peak, as has happened in many individual countries like the USA, the scale of the oil disruption would be not only little short of apocalyptic, but permanent.

What is driving the oil pincer is the huge increase in demand brought about by the extremely rapid industrialisation of the leading developing countries, above all China and India, but also embracing Brazil, Indonesia, Mexico, South Africa, Nigeria and many others following. Since China and India alone contain two-fifths of the entire world population and have until the current global slowdown maintained economic growth rates of 7–12 per cent a year for a decade, the demand that they exert on the world oil supply would rapidly have produced a global supply deficit even if the increasing fall in the number and size of new oilfield discoveries was not leading to a supply crunch anyway. But the rapidity and persistence of the Sino-Indian industrialisation growth rate has sharply accelerated the speed at which peak oil will be reached. Indeed, the International Energy Agency's 2008 World Energy Outlook states that without extra investment to raise production, the natural rate of output decline is now 9.1 per cent a year, and even with investment it is 6.4 per cent. These are far higher rates of decline than previously thought.

The dislocation caused by the growing shortfall in oil availability is likely to be on a scale unprecedented in human history. Our whole civilisation and our whole economy is based overwhelmingly on oil – not only industry, agriculture and transportation, but military capability too. Oil has been the key resource which has sustained the six-fold increase in world population over the last 150 years. James Lovelock, former NASA engineer and founder of the Gaia theory of the earth's evolution, believes that when the oil runs out within some forty to fifty years, the global human population will crash by up to 90 per cent.

Nor are there any alternatives to oil which are commercially, technically and environmentally viable. Perhaps the best hope of ameliorating the post-peak decline of world oil supply lies in the Athabaskan tar sands of western Canada, which some have compared to a new Saudi Arabia-like El Dorado, with enormous resources estimated to exceed 1,700 Gb (billion barrels), about a quarter of which might be recoverable by conventional methods. But the project fails on all three counts – it requires an oil price above $90 a barrel to be commercially viable, when the wild see-sawing of the oil price over recent years from $147 in 2007 to $40 in 2008 fatally undermines investor confidence. Technically, it requires colossal amounts of water which are rapidly draining the aquifers, and perhaps nuclear power to fuel the plants since local gas deposits are fast facing depletion. And environmentally, the enormous greenhouse gas emissions generated would produce a massive turbo climate change impact when world governments are increasingly committed to an 80 per cent reduction in such emissions by 2050.

Nevertheless, despite further equally strong objections to them, it would be unwise to write off other escape routes from the end of conventional oil, including shale oils, oil from coal, the viscous heavy oils of the Orinoco belt of eastern Venezuela, deep-water oil and polar oil. The constraints on oil supply over the past decade may have been more related to money than geology. Now that the current cost of Brent crude is $95 a barrel, $1 trillion has been invested in new oil in the two years 2010–11, and $600 billion is on course to be spent in 2012, mostly in Iraq but also more surprisingly in the US. One estimate suggests the Bakken shales in North Dakota contain almost as much oil as Saudi Arabia, though less of it can be extracted,[29] and this is only one of twenty such deposits in the US. This suggests that peak oil, while a valid concept ignored at our peril, may be much further off than widely believed.

The longevity of global gas supply will certainly be greater than that of oil, though not by a large margin. Total world production so far stands at about 2,700 tcf (trillion cubic feet), and the authoritative register 'Reported Proved Reserves' adds a further 6,350 tcf, though some of this lies in deep-water and polar regions and up to a quarter lies in Russia and former Soviet Union countries. Currently world production stands at 97 tcf a year, and it is reasonable to forecast that this may increase at 3 per cent a year to reach a plateau at about 125 tcf a year lasting from 2025 to 2040, followed by an annual decline of perhaps 5 per cent.

Again, some extension of these timelines may be achieved

29   Monbiot, G., *Guardian*, 3 July 2012.

by non-conventional gases, including coal-bed methane, gas shales, methane hydrates and natural gas liquids. Their potential resources are very large, but extraction is slow, difficult and expensive. Nevertheless the development of horizontal drilling and the use of high-pressure fluids to crack open otherwise impermeable shales (hydraulic fracturing, or 'fracking') has lifted US natural gas production from shales from 4 per cent in 2005 to 23 per cent in 2012. Analysis of forty-eight shale-gas basins in thirty-two countries indicated recoverable reserves of 6,700 tcf, and even that excluded likely discoveries in the former USSR and the Middle East.[30] Thus the turning point of peak gas can still be foreseen, but considerably beyond many of today's estimates.

(2) CHRONIC AND GROWING WATER SHORTAGE

Over-exploitation of the planet is thus leading to the exhaustion within perhaps fifty to a hundred years of fossil fuels (excluding coal) which were only created over aeons of time extending to several hundred million years. Nothing can more powerfully demonstrate the utter non-sustainability of the current world order. Yet even more important than accelerating oil and gas depletion are looming water and food shortages. UN estimates forecast the global consumption of fresh water doubling every twenty years, and suggest that within the next twenty years between a third and a half of the world's population (2.5–3.5 billion people) will live in areas of severe water stress, particularly concentrated in the Middle East, north Africa, northern China, south-east Australia and western USA–Mexico.

The causes of water shortage are population growth, climate

---

30   *Economist*, 6 August 2011, p. 54.

change, wasteful agriculture and changing diets. Without a new green revolution, farmers will need 60 per cent more water to feed the two billion extra people who will be born between now and 2025. Climate change is desertifying and making arid vast swathes of croplands across the world. Agriculture uses three-quarters of the world's water; while most people drink up to 3 litres a day on average, it takes 2,000–5,000 litres to grow the food they eat. Changing diets exacerbate this further: it takes 2,000 litres of water to grow a kilo of vegetables, but 15,000 litres to produce a kilo of beef – and meat consumption is rising fast, particularly in China. This is further compounded by another current trend – the switch to biofuels. It takes over 9,000 litres of water to grow the soy for one single litre of biodiesel, and up to 4,000 litres for the corn to be transformed into a litre of bioethanol. Thus what is meant to alleviate a serious environmental problem (climate change) is making another, even more serious problem (water shortage) worse.

The impact of all of these factors together means that the world could be facing annual losses equivalent to the entire grain crops of India and the US combined, which produce 30 per cent of globally consumed cereals. Water shortage will therefore have a dramatic knock-on impact on global food supplies. A study in the US journal *Science* (January 2009) found that no less than half the world's population is likely to face severe food shortages by the end of the present century as rising temperatures take their toll on farmers' crops. In addition, the over-exploitation of the oceans by industrialised fishing has drastically reduced the supply of fish, a key source of the world's protein. Nearly 50 per cent of all fish stocks are fully exploited, 20 per cent are over-exploited, and only 2 per cent are recovering.

(3) POPULATION OVER-DEMAND ON EARTH'S RESOURCES

Behind all these intensified pressures on the planet's finite resources lies the inexorable rise in world population. After the end of the last Ice Age about 11,000 years ago, which had lasted nearly 100 millennia, the global population grew slowly and reached about four million at the zenith of the Roman Empire. It then took nearly 2,000 years to reach one billion around 1800, but then only 125 years to reach two billion. After the Second World War it expanded exponentially, from 2.5 billion in 1950 to the present 7.0 billion, an increase of a billion in just fourteen years on average. It is now expected by the UN to reach 9.2 billion by 2050, an increase of a billion at only the slightly slower rate of every seventeen years. By any standards at all, this is simply unsustainable.

The key message from these facts and forecasts is that the human race has chronically overshot the capacity of its biosphere, the earth, to service it. We have almost become our own geophysical cycle. Our biological carbon productivity is outpaced only by the krill in the oceans. Our civil engineering works shift more soil each year than all the world's rivers bring down to the seas. Our industrial emissions now eclipse the total emissions from all the world's volcanoes. We are bringing about a species loss of biodiversity on a scale of some of the mass extinctions of palaeo-history. We are transforming the nitrogen cycle, adding more to the rainfall than is added by agriculture. And in the remotest parts of the world, trace contaminants like lead and DDT appear in the natural food chain (including polar bears in the Arctic).

Ecological footprint analysis indicates that the world human population hit the limits of planetary capacity about twenty years ago, at about the same time as per capita food production and world grain stocks began to shrink. Since then the human race has been in 'overshoot', currently taking out some 25 per cent more resources than the earth can renewably provide, a level of excess predicted to rise to about 80 per cent by mid-century. The WWF pamphlet 'Living Planet Report' has neatly encapsulated this idea, saying that within fifty or so years, at current rates of over-exploitation, we will require two earths. Some have argued that humanity has been in overshoot since the dawn of agriculture 10,000 years ago, and has survived only by 'mining' its soils, with the vast nutrient store contained in soils representing (like fossil fuels) a unique and unrepeatable asset that has been hugely depleted by accelerating agricultural erosion. Then, without petroleum and as the 'mining' of arable soils is forced to slow, the earth may only support a sustainable population of under 1.5 billion, an 80 per cent reduction on current levels.

However, just as Malthus drew attention in the eighteenth century to the 'positive checks' of war, famine and disease to keep overpopulation under control, so natural forces will certainly intervene again to restore earth and its human occupants to a new equilibrium. This time the central drivers will be energy shortages, water and food scarcity and sharply falling per capita access to resources, as well as climate change upheaval. This is a turning point of unparalleled magnitude in history when never before has a resource as critical as oil headed into initial decline and ultimate exhaustion from natural depletion without sight of a viable and equally flexible substitute. Without a fundamental change of strategy, however, the disappearance of oil will not neatly result in a hydrogen economy, renewables-generated electricity or fuel-cell-driven transportation. The political muscle of the fossil fuel industries is much more likely to shift policy towards a transitional gas-based bridge economy, supplemented by CCS (carbon capture and storage), coal and some expansion of nuclear.

However, there are severe drawbacks to all these options. World gas supply will decline steadily in the second half of this century, and Russia and Iran as two of the world's largest three repositories seem likely within a short time to prioritise their own domestic needs to the exclusion of foreign purchasers. CCS is an unproven technology, with no prototype currently existing anywhere in the world, an efficiency rating in sequestrating carbon of no more than 90 per cent, and a cost that may prove prohibitive without large public subsidies. And nuclear, while low in carbon emissions (from uranium mining and plant construction), has never overcome its inherent risks from colossal quantities of highly toxic nuclear waste, exposure to cancer and leukaemia clusters, catastrophic industrial accident and international nuclear proliferation. There must be a better way – and there is.

(4) GLOBAL WARMING AND THE CLIMATE CRUNCH

Another untenable dimension of the current world economic and technological order is that it is unleashing such drastic extremes in the climate as to put at risk within two to three centuries the survival of the human species. That the world is steadily warming is not in contention. The only issue that is disputed, and that by a very small minority, is what is causing it. Does it represent anything more than the natural variability of the climate, and is it serious enough to require a fundamental shift in human civilisations? The answer to both, based on the overwhelming weight of the evidence, is yes, but the response by governments across the world has so far been glacial.

The theory of global warming is that the sun's rays which have previously bounced off the earth back into space are increasingly trapped in the lower atmosphere by a layer of greenhouse gases (mainly carbon dioxide, but also methane and nitrous oxide, plus very small amounts of extremely potent hydrofluorocarbons, perfluorocarbons and sulphur hexafluoride) and reflected back to earth. The concentration of these greenhouse gases in the atmosphere, which was about 280 parts per million (ppm) prior to the start of industrialisation in the mid-eighteenth century, is now 387 and rising by 1–2 ppm per year. The UN Intergovernmental Panel on Climate Change, underpinned by 2,000–3,000 of the world's leading scientists, believes that when the threshold of 450 ppm is reached, the world is entering, climatically, an unpredictable danger zone. This scenario is challenged by a small group of scientists, many associated with Exxon Mobil, who argue that the theory does not precisely fit the observed facts in the short term (which is true – the theory still needs further refinement), though there is a remarkably close lock-step between atmospheric greenhouse gas ppm concentrations and global temperatures over the long term (the last half-million years).

Over recent years scientists across the world have reported compelling evidence, *inter alia*, of the runaway melting of Arctic sea ice, a much faster than expected slowdown of the global circulation systems in the north Atlantic, massive methane releases from melting permafrost in Siberia and Alaska, more violent hurricanes everywhere, and mega-droughts from northern China to the American West. Already, the WHO reckons, conservatively, some 200,000–300,000 people die each year worldwide from the impacts of climate change, notably malaria, dysentery and malnutrition – over 100 times the number who died in the Twin Towers attack.

In a single globalised world nobody is immune from these convulsions. A recent UN report has warned that rising sea levels, desertification and shrinking fresh water supplies will create up to 50 million environmental refugees by the end of this decade. If the ocean pumps around Greenland falter, northern European temperatures will plummet to those of Siberia. The London School of Hygiene and Tropical Medicine estimates that out of ten of the world's most dangerous vector-borne diseases, nine will increase their coverage across the world because of climate disruption. As the Greenland and Antarctic ice sheets melt, rising sea levels will threaten coastal cities worldwide, including London, as well as nuclear power stations and chemical waste dumps sited in coastal areas. Food supplies worldwide will be disrupted by intensifying droughts, and industrial agriculture will be particularly vulnerable to a surge in pathogens and pests from warmer temperatures.

But what is really worrying is that climate catastrophe is still only in its very early stages and that it is not a linear, but a dynamic, process of intensification. The very real risk is that at certain 'tipping points' dangerous runaway feedback effects of enormous power could abruptly generate a truly massive surge in carbon release (as has happened at previous mass extinctions) and ratchet up climate convulsion unpredictably. These include the dieback of the Amazon rainforest as soon as 2050, the release of billions of tons of methane hydrates from the ocean bed as the seas steadily warm, and the weakening of carbon sinks as forests, seas and soils lose their ability to absorb CO_2.

(5) THE POLITICS OF CLIMATE DESTRUCTION

Why then is so little being done when the scientific evidence is so stark and when the threat to the human race is so apocalyptic? The

Kyoto Protocol of 1997, the most comprehensive intergovernmental treaty achieved so far, was ratified by only thirty-two industrialised countries out of the world total of 190 and (so far) excludes
the US as well as China, India, Brazil and all the other developing
countries. Moreover, its target for signatory countries to reduce
greenhouse gas emissions by a mere 5 per cent by 2010 compared
to a 1990 baseline is vastly short of what the scientists assert is
necessary to stabilise the climate: a cut of at least 80 per cent by
2050. In the absence of far, far greater action to reduce greenhouse
gas emissions than has so far been taken worldwide, the world faces
not a 5 per cent cut in emissions, but a lethal increase of 75 per cent,
which would generate irreversibly destructive climate turmoil.

Despite climate destruction representing the most serious
overriding threat to the human race in its 150,000-year history,
the forces of resistance and denial remain extraordinarily strong.
There are several reasons for this. The Bush alliance with the US
oil industry, the view of almost all the developing countries that
ending poverty is more important than fighting climate change,
and the lack of inspired and determined political leadership
almost everywhere have all played their part. But the fundamental underlying constraint has been the iron grip, till now, of
the neo-liberal financial agenda with its unremitting emphasis
on untrammelled markets, endless growth, competitiveness,
deregulation and the enhancement and strengthening of Western
global power around the Washington consensus.

But all those factors are now changing. Obama is clearly
committed to a global climate change deal, and seems ready,
despite some slip-backs, to take on the US fossil fuel industries.
China and India are already, without signing up to the Kyoto
Protocol, taking extensive action to curb emissions, driven partly

by political fears that China could be a major victim of the ravages of climate change and partly by rebellion over hugely polluted Chinese cities. Political leadership is still feeble, but the huge increase in public awareness and the pain and fear produced by the increasing frequency and ferocity of extreme weather conditions – especially if more Katrina-type hurricanes savage the wealthy rather than the poor – is gradually pushing this issue higher up the political agenda.

But by far the most important change lies in the collapse of the neo-liberal financialised world order in the 2007–13 meltdown. Plummeting demand in the wake of the credit crunch has resulted in the enforced slowing of the hectic pell-mell pace of industrial exploitation of the planet's resources, and hence the slowing of the rate of global greenhouse gas emissions, opening the way to the construction of a rather different world system with significantly altered dynamics. For the last thirty years, and to a lesser degree before that, the dominant ideology of unfettered markets has overridden every other consideration, whether political, social or environmental. But the sudden jarring halt to this process is exposing hidden detriments which have long existed but which were ignored or dismissed because the central dynamic of the system seemed unstoppable. Such detriments certainly include the ill effects of ballooning inequality at both domestic and international levels, the dangerous competitiveness over shrinking energy and other natural resources that could lead to war, and the risks of pushing the international economic system over the threshold where climate catastrophe becomes irreversible.

The extent to which these are heeded will of course depend on the balance of power between the hitherto prevailing political–financial nexus and the new emergent forces in the wake of the global economic breakdown, the deepest and longest-lasting since the 1930s. The latter forces embrace a new multipolar global power system centred particularly round a US–China dyarchy, the ending of the Washington consensus as the arbiter of international economic rules, a more pronounced assertiveness of the poorer semi-industrialised countries on the world stage, an international determination to end the excesses of rampant financialisation of the economy, and a growing but still insufficient awareness of the risks to the planet from environmental cataclysm.

The net effect of these new forces could have been displayed at the Copenhagen world summit on climate change in December 2009, with a groundbreaking planetary climate deal between the US and China which could sufficiently tighten carbon reduction targets to place the world plausibly on track for an 80 per cent reduction by 2050 as well as agreeing key mechanisms to achieve it. It could have set the world on a radically new economic path which shifted the balance from virtually unencumbered exploitation of planetary resources, accompanied by virtually unchecked emissions, to a much more constrained balance between industrialisation and preservation of the biosphere. The almost comprehensive failure of the summit to achieve any such settlement illustrates starkly how resistant are the forces of power politics and economic self-interest in the major parties, especially China and the US, to making what might be seen as even the smallest concessions to an international common interest. As a result, action to combat climate turmoil in future is likely to be delivered not via enormous international jambo-rees but by individual countries voluntarily offering their own contributions (as all the main countries did in the weeks before Copenhagen), provided, of course, they are then carried through.

A return to intergovernmental parleying is perhaps only likely in the face of a series of unprecedented climate catastrophes across the globe which put a much higher premium on common concerted action. That could still well happen as the ravages of climate change intensify.

The other major driver which could yet salvage systematic anti-climate change activity is a Green New Deal, driven less by conversion to the risks to human survival than by a plausible plan for the reconstruction of the world economy. Such a programme, which is gradually gaining more political traction, would aim to close down the world's fossil fuel industries as quickly as was feasible, launch a massive drive worldwide for a rapid and comprehensive switch to renewable sources of energy, incentivise energy conservation at every level and phase in a much lower utilisation of mineral and other natural resources either through household carbon quotas or through a new environmentally calibrated currency.

Markets will not, of course, disappear; they will simply play a distinctly different role – one of negotiation, where the parameters are set by an alternative dynamic. Whereas carbon trading and carbon offsets, within the UN-CDM (Clean Development Mechanism) and EU-ETS (Emissions Trading Scheme) systems, have purloined the environmental search for market solutions and transformed them into bankable carbon credits with little or no benefit to the planet, the need now is for a much tighter regulatory framework – whatever, in fact, the biosphere requires for its viability – and allowing market mechanisms to operate strictly and exclusively within those boundaries. That may well require a World Environmental Court to ensure that the new rules are fully and fairly implemented as a prior

jurisdiction, before the World Trade Organization is author-
ised to resolve disputes at the consequential commercial level.
That will be one essential component as the new world order
takes shape.

CHAPTER IV

VALUES: THE COMMERCIALISATION OF LIFE

There is a common link within Britain between economic decline, the fracturing of society and the neglect of environmental over-exploitation, as set out in the preceding three chapters. That link lies with the ever greater application of the values of free market capitalism to all areas of the economy, society and the environment, and this in turn has stemmed from the unchallenged dominance of the financial elite.

(I) THE GLORIFICATION OF WEALTH

The core British values of tolerance, instinctive liberalism, communal support for well-understood social values, belief in fairness, respect for parliamentary democracy, responsible internationalism and a strong sense of national purpose and history have steadily dissipated in the teeth of relentless individualism, indifference and even hostility to the disadvantaged, and at times even rampant xenophobia. The commitment to social justice, altruism and a belief in overriding moral values has been displaced by a strident worship of wealth, bling and celebrity. This has happened increasingly over the last three decades because the values of the wider society have been assimilated to those of the corporate and financial elite. An almost exponential explosion of income and wealth in the topmost stratum of Western society, most notably in the US and UK, is justified on the grounds that it is 'fair' – the doctrine that the super-rich deserve whatever they have. Conversely, the poor, in their view and that of the virulently right-wing media, largely deserve their plight because they could have made a different 'lifestyle choice' – to work, save and show some initiative. Morality and emotive understanding have been coarsened, and whatever towering inequalities the underlying economic system has thrown up are treated as the natural and normal order of things, justly separating the deserving from the undeserving in terms of character and worth. The question is never asked, let alone any answer attempted, as to whether the economic system itself is profoundly unfair and the inordinate differences in wealth, status and power reflect not inherent worth but rather the differential opportunity to exploit the self-indulgence and greed permitted by the system at the top.

That self-indulgence is perhaps greater than at any other time in modern history, and is justified by endless rationalisations. 'Greed is good' pronounced Michael Milken, the Wall Street junk bond king, before he was sent to jail. Sky-high bonuses are, it is said, necessary to retain the best, and thus ensure the health of an industry from which the whole country benefits, ignoring the fact that the bankers had just nearly brought the entire economy to its knees. The paradox is played out repeatedly that the rich need to be exorbitantly rewarded in order to get the best out of them while the poor have to be kept low paid, otherwise they will lose the will to work. The all-important principle of 'fairness' has been up-ended so that a one-off tax on bank bonuses in December 2009 was derided as 'not fair' even though it was a small contribution to clearing up the mess the bankers had themselves created. The idea of fairness has lost all objective underpinning, and is deployed simply as a rhetorical device to justify their status as an overpaid financial elite.

There are several disturbing consequences of this transformation of capitalism whereby chief executives as mere officers of their corporations have, for the first time in history, become enormously rich without having to risk any money of their own. Richard Lambert, former director general of the CBI, noted in April 2010 they were so extravagantly remunerated that they now occupied a different galaxy from the rest of us, and risked becoming aliens in their own communities. Some of the earlier protagonists of capitalism (e.g. Ove Arup or John Lewis) understood all too well that personal rewards had to remain proportional and profits had to deliver wider social goals than merely maximising shareholder value. But capitalism in its neo-liberal extreme has arrived at a moral dead end, increasingly focused on feathering the nests of its leaders while imposing enormous costs on the rest of society and accepting no reciprocal obligations.

(2) THE APOTHEOSIS OF MARKETS

The worship of wealth has been taken to such exorbitant extremes over the last three decades because the Washington consensus, the mantra of neo-liberal capitalism, dictated that markets should be unfettered to the fullest degree feasible, finance deregulated, state functions privatised wherever possible and the role of the state minimised to its core functions of defence, foreign policy, law and order, and taxation, leaving self-regulating markets to do the rest. Markets, it was said, are naturally more efficient and innovative, while the state is all too often bureaucratic, politically riven and mired in a bog of contesting interests. Wealth creation, which was taken to be the central goal of modern societies, would be optimised by giving markets maximum freedom and conversely keeping governments and the public sector from meddling, which would only undermine the most efficient allocation of resources.

Experience, however, told a very different story. Deregulated financial markets spun out of control as a result of the sub-prime fiasco in 2008 and effectively ruined many of the biggest banks on Wall Street, in the City of London and across the Western world. They were only saved from bankruptcy by massive taxpayer bail-outs which only the state could orchestrate. The neo-classical balanced-budget policies then pursued by so many Western countries in the wake of the crash, prompted by powerful pressures from the markets despite their culpability for the financial crisis in the first place, have produced a prolonged stagnation likely to endure until 2015. The only escape will come when a large-scale public sector-driven jobs and growth strategy is set in place to lay the foundations for restoring aggregate demand which can then kick-start a recovery of the private sector. Only the state has the power and resources to do that. Equally, only the state, in collaboration with other states, has the authority to drive through policies to slow down and reverse climate change, to ensure necessary long-term energy investment, and to lay down the rules to prevent over-exploitation of the planet and ensure the survival of an ecosystem which can maintain the human race.

The lionising of the market and its products has generated an era of unabashed consumer materialism. The market, for all its failings and limitations, is seen as the measure of all things. If something gains approval in the market, however trivial, irrelevant or amoral it might seem, that proves it is successful and worthwhile. If no one had their market opportunity blocked, the result, it is argued, however unfair it might look, should be accepted as fair. Yet the outcome of a competitive process can only properly be regarded as fair if the starting line is genuinely equal for all and not, as at present, heavily loaded in favour of those with existing wealth, power, networks and resources, and also if all participants have a broadly equal chance.[31]

(3) THE COMMERCIALISATION OF VALUE

The concentration on markets as the universal panacea has led to the relentless commercialisation of all aspects of human life. The network of wider social relationships within tightly knit communities has unravelled in the face of an aggressive economic individualism which marginalised co-operative values and mutual support. Personal and financial insecurity has been on the increase, partly because average real incomes have stagnated over the last thirty years, but also because of the widespread decline in voluntary, community and charitable organisations,[32] a process accelerated by the 2010–15 spending cuts. The assumption of greed and narrow self-interest as the only reliable drivers is destructive; it undermines the higher-level motivators such as pride in work, the desire to be useful, self-expression and a sense of belonging, as well as the ethical standards of professionalism.

Under market economics human advance is measured in terms of growth of GDP, but that is not the same as welfare. The problem with gross domestic product is precisely that it is 'gross'[33] – there are no deductions involved: all economic activity is accounted for as if it were of positive value. Car crashes which

---

31 Not, for example, if one or more contestants have only one leg.

32 'Strategies against Poverty', Joseph Rowntree Foundation, December 2004.

33 Dasgupta, Sir P., 'Nature's Role in Sustaining Economic Development', *Philosophical Transactions of the Royal Society B*, January 2010.

generate motor repairs, medical work and funeral costs are on this analysis as beneficial as car production. Health, quality of life and inequality play no part in its measurement. Even more importantly, no deduction is made to account for the depreciation of natural capital – the overuse or degradation of soil, water, forests, fisheries and the atmosphere. Indeed, the total wealth of a nation can decline even as its GDP is growing, a condition that has applied to several Western countries in recent years. Conversely, Japan has now experienced two decades of flat-lining GDP, yet its living standards are among the highest in the world – its unemployment is half that of the US, its life expectancy five years longer, its average real incomes are the same as Germany's and its inequality lower.

(4) THE AMORALITY AND GREED OF NEO-LIBERALISM

The riots of August 2011 laid bare the underlying dynamics of the economic system. Taking advantage, squeezing every last bit out of the system, illegally if necessary, without any regard for the effect on everyone else – because you can – has now become endemic at all levels of society. The bankers did it by deliberately misselling sub-prime mortgages to Ninja people (no income, no jobs or assets), but securitising them – trading them on around the world – allowing the bankers to make huge profits before the roof fell in. MPs took advantage of the expenses system, even fraudulently switching their designated second home to enlarge their gains. Big corporations set up the most dense and impenetrable chains of companies to avoid tax and to maximise the use of tax havens. Newspapers used massive-scale phone-hacking, a criminal activity, to keep ahead of rivals with scoops on celebrities and to drive up their sales, even abusing the public trust (and the law) in the most degrading manner. In each it's help your-self to it, whether 'it' is mega-bonuses for bankers or branded goods for looters, wherever you can. The rioters were no different except they had no internal system that they privately controlled to exploit, only the public domain.

Greed has always been inherent in capitalist systems, but the (relatively) balanced capitalism that prevailed in the quarter-century after the war (1948–73) involved the idea of a social contract and at least a limited sense of responsibility for each other in communities. That was steadily squeezed out by the unchained, deregulated, free-for-all neo-liberal version of capi-talism in the 1980s, 1990s and 2000s. The concept of a social contract and a moral responsibility to each other was discarded as old fashioned, and replaced by a dog-eat-dog mentality, a ruthless and uncaring individualism. With the financial crash of 2008–9, the breakdown of the US economy, the persisting eurozone crisis, the prolonged stagnation in the global economy, and anti-austerity riots in several European countries, including (though for partly different reasons) Britain, this system reached a nadir of political and economic collapse in the elongated and deepening recession of 2009–14. Talk of inculcating a proper sense of moral responsibility as the antidote to unrest on the streets, while leaving intact the underlying system that generates it in the first place, is to misunderstand the dynamics of the crisis.

Even the boom of the previous decade, while it lasted, was the product of a non-durable housing bubble and unsustain-able levels of private debt. Neo-liberal 'modernisation' created unaccountable monopolies of capital, along with a centralis-ing, micro-managing and increasingly authoritarian state. Its enterprise culture, flexible labour market and marketised welfare reform all generated insecurity, anxiety and isolation. Kindness, care and generosity were out of keeping with the dominant market culture, and the ideal of public service was constantly denigrated. These are not the values and principles chosen by the mass of people, but the social consequences of a system holding them in its grip as its internal economic dynamics are remorselessly played out to their logical conclusion. Turning that round requires both deep moral conviction and intense political determination to engineer a series of profound reforms in financial and corporate governance, the role of markets and the state, company ownership, remuneration systems and worker representation. As yet, there is little sign of any such transformation.

(5) SPIRITUAL EMPTINESS AND LOSS OF DIRECTION AND PURPOSE

While some detect a growing sense of *fin de siècle*, it certainly seems a deeper malaise has set in, driven not merely by fear and bitterness at unprecedented austerity, but more profoundly still by a rapid succession of traumatic blows to the nation's sense of identity. There has been a dramatic loss of confidence in the authority of the country's leaders – the selfishness and arrogance of the financial elite, the politicians' expenses scandal and blatant breaking of promises, and the culpability and excesses of a sensationalistic media that has corrupted both police and governments. Accountability has been weakened in all walks of life, and the checks and balances – the foundation of a democratic system – have all but disappeared. A devastating stream of WikiLeaks has exposed the regular hypocrisy and manipulativeness of governments.

There is a pervasive sense of drift, with the previous certainties of religious authority replaced by iconoclastic secularism and shallow materialism which are neither satisfying nor meaning-ful. An unfettered market has shredded the bonds of communal solidarity and individual altruism. Ideological convictions have been corroded in the face of demands for winning and hold-ing onto power, with an extraordinary lack of vision displayed once power has been secured. And a mindless but ever pervasive consumerism has dumbed down much of the spirit of creativity, innovation and renewal. What is now needed more than anything is a revived sense of ideological direction, a belief in a more profound cause wider and deeper than self and personal enrichment, and a reconnection of political purpose with an encompassing and fulfilling vision.

A sense of national identity and purpose is dangerously lack-ing. An anguished debate about Britishness and multiculturalism betrays the loss of inner self-confidence. The subordination of all economic assets to the international marketplace, even those vital to the nation's survival, has allowed the sale of key compo-nents of the nation's economic infrastructure in a manner which no other government would tolerate, especially when it is not reciprocated. Talk of English or British nationalism is seen as at best jingoistic and at worst racist. Children are not taught British history at school in a manner which endows a strong and clear cultural sense of what being British means.

Above all, a spiritual emptiness in the West is almost palpa-ble. The decline of binding moral imperatives has given way to a culture which is increasingly shallow, ephemeral and often trivial. The commercialisation of everything has robbed life of much of its deeper meaning and created a chasm that separates acquisitiveness from happiness. As against this moral, social and spiritual loss of purpose, what is now desperately needed

is a political culture that values the social goods that give security, meaning and value to people: home, family, friendships,
rewarding work, locality and communities of belonging – the
reinvention of a modern, plural and ethical socialism.

A DYSFUNCTIONAL POWER STRUCTURE RESISTANT TO CHANGE

The link that brings together the ills spelt out in the last chapter lies with the power-brokers who have condoned these consequences for their own purposes. Britain is run by the elites in finance, business, the media and politics, and each of them has failed profoundly in their role to contribute towards producing a viable, sustainable and harmonious society. They have chosen instead to maximise their own interests to the intense detriment of the wider public interest. Until that structure is radically overhauled and replenished by a very different power system focused relentlessly on the conditions needed for the sustainable revival of Britain, this country will not escape from its slow but, on current trends, irrevocable decline.

(I) THE DESTRUCTIVENESS OF BUSINESS AS USUAL IN THE CITY

The causes of the 2008–9 financial crash were multiple. An overlax monetary policy encouraged an excessive leveraging culture. Extreme light-touch regulation left too much to the markets. A vast global market was created in credit derivatives that were not well understood but were recklessly securitised across the world because of their high profitability. The selling frenzy was stoked by enormous bonuses which drove the recklessness. The banking structure was so over-concentrated in the lead banks that when disaster struck, they were judged too big to fail, with catastrophic consequences for both the national debt and the budget deficit. And the business model linked speculative investment with retail deposit-taking, with the former as well as the latter protected by an implicit taxpayer guarantee. All these causes need to be dealt with, yet none has been, both because of the intransigence of the banking lobby against any reform and because of the weakness of political supervision, making another financial crash almost inevitable, when it might well prove impossible to persuade taxpayers to fund a second massive bail-out.

Derivatives – particularly credit default swaps, a £65 trillion market, and collateralised debt obligations – are a perennial candidate for triggering the next crisis since they add opacity and leveraging to the financial system. The key regulatory measure is transparency, which the US Dodd–Frank Act sought to achieve by requiring all derivatives to be traded across public exchanges. Some highly dubious securities had gained a spurious status in the UK through the scandal of credit-rating agencies which were paid by the very institutions whose creditworthiness they were supposed to be assessing. That should be made illegal; better still, the function should be transferred to the public sector in order to ensure integrity and transparency. Equally, there is public outrage that a banking system that owes its continued existence to massive government intervention should still pay itself mega-salaries and bonuses, and that 90 per cent of investment bank profits in an age of austerity are directed not at strengthening balance sheets nor at shareholder dividends nor at lower fees for customers, but at gigantic personal pay-offs. While Whitehall has argued that demands by other countries (e.g. France) for a mandatory cap and a removal of any guarantee for bonuses is impractical, there can be no doubt that if the G20 governments insisted on limits and made continued liquidity provisions dependent on compliance, no bank could refuse.

To avert future financial crises, too much emphasis has been placed on enhancing capital controls, but in a manner and degree unlikely to be effective. At the outset of the 2008–9 financial crisis virtually all financial institutions across the globe had capital adequacy at least equal to the minimum Basel regulatory requirements and in some cases twice as much. Despite the near-global collapse under these provisions, Basel III, the latest ground rules laid down by the world's leading bankers, proposed in 2010 that the core top-tier capital requirement should be only 4.5 per cent of total lending, and the contingency capital requirement only 2.5 per cent. Of the EU's top fifty banks, forty-five already met that standard, and Basel III did not even require these new provisions to come into force till 2019. This is far too little, too late, reflecting governments' connivance with the banks in minimising reform. Much better would be counter-cyclical capital controls, enforcing different levels of bank capital at different stages in the economic cycle, though that would of course leave open contention about the degree of ratchet and the timing of it.

An alternative approach would be to introduce in Britain something like the Volcker rule, restricting banks from undertaking certain kinds of speculative trading, notably proprietary trading. But that would still not overcome the 'too big to fail' problem when applied to investment banks – it wouldn't, for example, have prevented the collapse of Lehman Brothers. The problem, too, which applies to the Vickers Commission's proposals, is that any rule-based reform faces the risk of regulatory arbitrage because financial institutions invent ever more sophisticated products simply geared to get round regulatory controls. That is the case for splitting retail high street banking from investment casino banking. The key advantage would be that it would remove the implicit taxpayer guarantee which at present allows financial conglomerates safely to use retail deposits for proprietary trading. However, the counter to that argument is that if the failure of a financial institution outside the narrow banking boundary threatened systemic contagion, it is difficult to believe that the government would not attempt some form of bail-out. There must be doubt therefore whether the narrow banking model can by itself be relied upon to overcome the problems of moral hazard and 'too big to fail'.

An alternative, however, recently mooted – the Kotlikoff proposal in the US – might succeed in achieving this objective. The core of the model is that all financial companies become pass-through mutual funds. They would have a 100 per cent equity ratio to guarantee bank solvency, and the payments function of banks would be performed by cash funds that would be 100 per cent reserve, e.g. through Treasury bonds. Such banks could, of course, still initiate new mortgages and new loans, but these would not be funded through deposit accounts until they had been sold to a mutual fund. The key point is that the bank would never hold them, i.e. it would never have an open position. Banks would not own assets, apart from their offices and physical equipment, and they would not then be in a position to fail or trigger a bank run. For those who want to take greater risks beyond a cash-based mutual fund, there are of course hundreds of investment avenues that would continue to be available, such as foreign exchange, real estate, hedge funds and all the rest. The key difference with this limited-purpose banking would be that any failure in such investments would be incurred by the investor, not by the bank.

In the absence of any significant reform, Britain retains the most profoundly dysfunctional banking system of any G7 country. It came nearer to collapse than any other in the autumn of 2008. There is a need to break up the mega-banks with their addiction to mortgage lending. Britain needs smaller banks and in particular specialist business banks such as infrastructure banks, housing banks, green banks, creative industries banks, and knowledge economy banks. Only such a fundamental reform, in terms of structure, size and operational practice, can deliver the banking system needed for a regenerated and sustainable British economy.

(2) MEGA-CORPORATIONS THAT FAIL BRITAIN

Britain's industry has also failed in several ways to provide the foundations for a sustainable and viable economy. First, the emphasis has been strongly on growth via mergers and acquisitions rather than new investment, with company takeovers quadrupling over the last fifteen years while fixed investment by industrial and commercial companies has stagnated. It is perhaps the starkest indicator of Britain's distorted corporate priorities. Management so often continues to grow companies not by innovation and creating new products or better services, but by taking over the competition. Shareholders, for their part, choose, when a company is in difficulty, not to focus on achieving a constructive reorganisation of the company, but too readily to sell out to the highest bidder. The fear of takeover then prompts all quoted companies to prioritise the share price by maximising short-term financial gains rather than long-term market share in order not to fall victim to potential predators. By the same token the barriers are raised against new investment, with higher rates of return demanded in the short term as well as payback periods being squeezed, so that companies are forced to treat their core skilled workforce not as a key foundation for long-term success but rather as a residual variable to adjust to changing economic vicissitudes.

Second, there is a readiness to embed the market principle, to a degree which no other country in Europe would contemplate, to wave through foreign takeovers even in key strategic sectors which might threaten the integrity of the national economy. German and French firms have snapped up British water and electricity companies, London's airports were taken over by Ferrovial, a Spanish construction consortium, and first the Dutch and then the Indians walked off with Britain's steel industry. The Chinese bought Rover, the rump of Britain's car industry, and shipped its machine tools back home. Dubai snapped up P&O, and BT – conveniently no longer called British Telecom – may well become the first 'national' telecoms incumbent to fall into foreign hands, since its mobile arm has already been taken over by Telefónica, a Spanish company. Similarly, BAE Systems – Britain's largest manufacturing company, but no longer British Aerospace – clearly looks to its future in the American defence market, no doubt in junior partnership with one of the US giants, Lockheed Martin, Northrop Grumman or Boeing.

The tragedy is that British scientists' and engineers' former world leadership in innovation in areas like jet engines and pharmaceuticals has been drawn into cooking up algorithms for hedge funds and investment banks where the profits (and potentially the losses) are far higher. Where UK manufacturing continues to thrive, it is often through inward direct investment such as Nissan's car factory in Sunderland. But elsewhere across the spectrum the acquisition of British assets in the 2000s has turned into a stampede. American equity investors eyed up Sainsbury's as the epitome of Britain's high street, and Nasdaq launched a furious battle to take over the bigger London stock exchange. Gigantic loans enabled Spanish corporations to purchase BAA, O₂ and Abbey National, the UK world leader in glass manufacture, Pilkingtons, was bought up by a small Japanese competitor, and the cornerstone of British technology, Smiths Electronics, disappeared into the US General Electric. More recently, in 2010 the iconic British company Cadbury's was allowed to fall into the hands of the US conglomerate Kraft, which immediately closed a Cadbury factory it had pledged not to, while in 2011 the UK government's handing the huge Thameslink contract to the German competitor Siemens will likely end train-making in Britain.

What is most disturbing is the lack of resistance. Managers and shareholders quietly acquiesce in a foreign bid, pocket the gains in the takeover package or share price, and depart with gentlemanly decorum. Such is the obsession with globalisation that damage to the long-term foundations of the British economy is scarcely questioned, nor the loss of British expertise, nor the likely decline in engineering jobs, increasingly taken by foreign nationals, nor even the direct consequences of loss of ownership. Thames Water, as an illustrative example, was bought by the German company RWE in 2000 for £4.3 billion, which then raised £1.4 billion in loans against the assets, depositing the proceeds in Germany while requiring the debt to be repaid by Thames's customers in London; that caused the Germans to resist making sufficient investment, either to ensure London was protected from droughts or to ensure that the extremely high leakage rate was addressed, until they sold the company to an Australian bank for £8 billion. Altogether foreigners have spent $1 trillion (£625 billion) on acquiring 5,400 British companies in the last decade.[34] The most obvious risks are factory closures and job losses, with Britain becoming a 'branch factory' as power shifts abroad. Foreign owners are more likely, when having to cut capacity, to chop factories far from home. High-value head office jobs and R&D skills will migrate abroad.

Britain is uniquely relaxed in its open market for corporate control. In the 1980s the US sought barriers against Japanese corporations taking over Hollywood and prime Manhattan property. In the 2000s Germany fretted that a swarm of 'locusts', mainly American, were devouring their prized industrial *Mittelstand*. France has notoriously blocked takeovers of its major national firms, even declaring a yogurt-maker a strategic asset against an American bid. The US itself still allows 'poison pill' defences against unwanted takeovers. In the EU, large family shareholdings, often with enhanced voting rights, together with the use of foundations and trust, protect companies from hostile bids. By comparison British business families more readily lose control because shareholdings can quickly become widely dispersed.

A third fundamental structural weakness in British industry is the break-up of its supply chains, which profitably connect the different competences of a diverse population of small, medium and giant enterprises which sell branded, finished goods. Broken supply chains and fragmented networks expose small players to the sourcing whims of the largest companies. British manufacturing

---

34   *Economist*, 27 March 2010.

has relatively few large corporate players with UK headquarters that have global reach, broad capabilities and a large workforce of over 50,000. Yet critically these are the companies that boost cost recovery by selling branded finished products, sustain civil R&D, build technological competences and connect backwards to domestic suppliers. The reasons Britain lacks these crucial chain-supporting enterprises are: the predominant concept of shareholder value irrespective of long-term market share; the break-up of giant manufacturing firms (e.g. GEC, ICI, Lucas, TI) assessed as inadequately profitable; and privatisations (e.g. rail and electric power) without regard to a domestic supplying industry.

Of those giant firms that remain, BAE Systems as national defence contractor now depends on military orders (having sold its stake in the Airbus consortium in 2006), GSK and AstraZeneca pharma companies rely heavily on aggressive marketing of intellectual property rights, and Rolls Royce is the UK's only large, world-class, high-tech champion which makes complex, high-value, finished products for civilian markets. In the rank below are a few publicly quoted firms such as Smiths Group and GKN as global suppliers of detection systems or car components with around 20,000 employees each, way ahead of such firms as JCB or Weir offering big brands in small market segments.[35]

Now that the big UK factories of the 1970s have been closed or sold off because of shareholder demands for greater profit or because inept privatisations destroyed crucial supply chains, the British manufacturing landscape as the legacy of Thatcherism and New Labour is now dominated by small workshops. CSO and

---

35   Froud, J., Johal, S., Law, J., Leaver, A. and Williams, K., 'Rebalancing the Economy (or Buyer's Remorse)', CRESC Working Party paper 87, January 2011.

ONS figures show that factories with over 200 employees have halved in the past twenty-five years: by 2008 there were fewer than 2,000 factories employing over 200, compared with 107,000 employing fewer than ten. UK-owned firms are therefore largely constrained in a workshop sector with little capacity to move up the supply chain. By contrast, foreign-owned firms in the UK have larger factories (an average of 200 employees), but they are mainly branch assembly plants limited in their ambition to expand and export by their corporate parent, for whom the UK is an important market, not the lowest-cost production base whose export profitability varies with dollar-to-pound fluctuations.

(3) A MEDIA THAT HAS LOST ITS REAL ROLE

It is not only Britain's finance and industrial sectors that have seriously compromised their true goals to advance their own interest against the national interest: its mass media have as well. To maintain a properly functioning democracy, the real objectives of the media should be twofold: firstly, to keep the electorate fully informed about the key issues that affect the nation and thus to provide a genuine national agenda, and secondly, to speak truth to power and thus to lay the foundations for systematically holding the government of the day to account. With some honourable exceptions Britain's media has fallen far short of these democratic responsibilities. Instead of offering without fear or favour an open mirror on Britain's society, it has partly used its key role to assert its own partisan power and to spread its own *parti pris* propaganda, and has partly degenerated into becoming a mindless purveyor of scandal, celebrity and sensationalism that may sell newspapers but degrades the national consciousness.

Almost no constraints are placed on private ownership of the press, it being used as a bauble of public power by which wealthy tycoons can seek to shape the world to suit their own interests. Britain imposes no nationality requirement. It only loosely controls the share of any media market held by any single proprietor. It does not limit cross-ownership between the print and broadcasting media. It does not regulate to prevent market dominance. It is merely assumed that lightly applied competition law together with self-regulation is all that is needed. As a result London's only evening newspaper is owned by a Russian oligarch, Alexander Lebedev, allegedly linked to the former KGB. Lebedev also part-owns the *Independent* titles, while Richard Desmond, the former pornographer, owns both the *Express* titles as well as Channel 5. The owners of the *Telegraph* titles, the Barclay brothers, are domiciled in the Channel Islands. And Rupert Murdoch, for the last three decades the most dominant force in British newspapers via his News International, was till recently also emerging as the foremost actor in British television through Sky, of which he controlled 39 per cent and bid for all the remainder, which would have given him no less cross-media power than Berlusconi's Mediaset.

There are serious drawbacks to this structure and composition of media governance. It allows far too much market share to power-hungry moguls whose ambitions often run counter to the public interest. Murdoch already commanded 37 per cent of the UK newspaper market via his ownership of *The Sun*, *The Times*, the *Sunday Times* and (until July 2011) the *News of the World*, and if he had obtained full control of BSkyB in addition to his News Corp base his enterprise would have been worth some £6.4 billion a year, nearly double the BBC's funding of £3.6 billion. It also narrows the range of ideological diversity since billionaire private owners tend to share a similar preponderant right-wing bias which reinforces the prevailing Establishment consensus and does not reflect at all the wide diversity of opinion in the electorate at large. More sinisterly, it enables proprietors to use the purported influence of their newspapers at election time to do secret deals with the Prime Minister which subvert the media laws and regulation of a parliamentary democracy. Thus Murdoch suborned a Tory government into letting him acquire *The Times* and *Sunday Times* on the flimsy grounds that there would be independent non-executive directors on the board, then leant on Thatcher to rescind the law prohibiting cross-ownership between print and broadcast media so that he could take over BSkyB, and finally had all but got his bid for total control of BSkyB waved through by the Tory government in 2011 as his price for switching to support the Tories at the 2010 election when the phone-hacking revelations at the *News of the World* torpedoed his takeover at the very last minute.

That scandal exposed how far the corrupting tentacles of media power stretched into the very core of the British Establishment. News International insisted for years that phone-hacking was the work of a single rogue reporter, only for it to be later revealed that the criminal activity of hacking was rife on an industrial scale, involving at least 4,000 victims. Scotland Yard had been sitting on 11,000 pages of evidence containing all the names for five years, but failed to take any action for fear of offending Murdoch. The politicians were in hock to the media magnate – Blair having flown to Australia in 1996 to pay fealty to the Murdoch court, Brown having failed to insist on a public inquiry into phone-hacking in 2009, and Cameron having had twenty-six meetings with News International executives in a fifteen-month period in 2010–11 when getting full control of

BSkyB was Murdoch's central objective. Parliament also was cowed into silence by the overt threat that if any MPs challenged the Murdoch empire, enough dirt would be dug up against them to trash their reputations in the Murdoch papers. Furthermore Murdoch had already made clear that his next objective was to end or override the BBC's role as public service broadcaster and to get the requirement for political balance in broadcasting lifted so that television would adopt a British version of his wildly partisan US Fox News.

This lust for dominance and control, in the tradition of Beaverbrook, Rothermere, Northcliffe, Cecil King and latterly Murdoch, has unsurprisingly meant that the true functions of the British media have been distorted out of all recognition. Instead of the press acting as independent assessor of government policy, the leading proprietor, commanding nearly 40 per cent of the market, was more of a political insider than members of the Cabinet: 'Rupert and Mrs Thatcher consult regularly on every important matter of policy' (according to Charles Douglas-Home, one of Murdoch's editors). Blair consulted Murdoch (often referred to as the twenty-fourth member of the Labour Cabinet or as second only to the PM himself) three times in February 2003 about the Iraq War. Murdoch himself testified that the politician he had most contact with was Brown. Instead of revealing hidden evidence and deploying argument in open debate, democracy was up-ended by proprietors' private meetings with the Prime Minister to fix secret deals undisclosed to the Cabinet, Parliament or the nation. Instead of the wide diversity of opinion getting a full airing, the prejudices of a tiny number of media oligarchs dominated, unhindered by any right of reply or by ease of access for new entrants in a tightly controlled market or by any standard of political balance. Instead of any serious attention being focused on holding the government of the day to account, tabloid journalism descended into prurience and scandal about the follies and fripperies of film stars, TV personalities and footballers, and assorted other extravagances. As a media with a crucial role in a democratic society, the British press has lost it.

(4) POLITICAL GOVERNANCE HAS BROKEN DOWN

Constitutionally the role of government, following a successful election, is to lead the conduct of the nation's affairs in accordance with the manifesto of the winning party, mediated by a Parliament primed to hold it to account in the performance of these functions. The reality has long since been utterly different. Elections have long been won far more on the personalities and presentation of the party leaders than on party manifestos, which hardly anyone reads. Solemn promises made to the electorate are regularly broken virtually with impunity. Parliament's role has been successively and cumulatively weakened ever since the time of Lloyd George, to the point where it has both lost the confidence of its electors and been regarded by some Prime Ministers with studied disdain.

Over the last thirty years in particular, instead of tightening scrutiny over executive excesses Parliament has become less ideological, more tribally loyalist, more careerist. It failed utterly to hold the Thatcher–Major governments to account over arms to Iraq, the Blair government over the Iraq war, and the Brown government over capitulation to the City. The recent reforms – setting up a backbench business committee and electing select committees – scarcely begin to redress the balance of power which has been drained away largely by the assertiveness of No. 10, by Thatcher's dominatrix model and by Blair's Napoleonic regime. Its power is continually seeping away to Brussels as the EU mandate spreads ever wider. And the judiciary increasingly encroaches on the parliamentary prerogative, no doubt prompted by the judges' view that if Parliament can't hold the executive to account, they will.

That central failing of Parliament, worse than the expenses scandal of 2009, dreadful though that was, is its current inability to provide the effective checks and balances against the growing appropriation of power by the executive. The scrutiny of bills is laborious but almost wholly ineffective since governments use their majority at every stage to vote down virtually all amendments irrespective of content. On matters of overarching national importance Parliament cannot set up its own committees of inquiry and is dependent on No. 10's willingness to do so, which on the most sensitive issues (e.g. currently on the corruption of public life exposed by the hacking scandal between banks, media, police, government and corporations, or on the causes of the riots) is usually not forthcoming. Where No. 10 does choose to do so, it is the Prime Minister, not Parliament, who chooses the chairman and members and determines the terms of reference, which can often angle the committee's deliberations in the direction the Prime Minister wants, even though it is usually the latter's record that is being investigated.

Effective representation of the people by the MPs they choose demands a string of other reforms too. Parliament should routinely carry out confirmation hearings, as in the US, of leading public sector and some ministerial appointments. It needs its own legal counsel if it is to be an effective check on executive power. It should be empowered to monitor and cross-examine large expenditure programmes at their formation, not just after the event, as currently happens, aided by a new cadre of expert external advisers. It should also require professional lobbyists to keep a public register including the scope of their activities, the source of all their funding and the details of their meetings with ministers. A limited number of key select committee reports should be debated and voted on the floor of the House, not, as at present, left to gather dust in the archives. And to bring Parliament closer to the people it represents, public petitions signed by a high threshold number of electors should also be automatically subject to debate and vote in the House, not just considered for debate, as is currently the case.

Paradoxically, while Parliament has been shorn of these powers it needs by the steadily growing centralisation of power within No. 10, the latter itself has been gravely weakened by the central tenet of its own ideology of neo-liberalism, namely that government should devolve power to the fullest degree feasible to the markets and withdraw to its own irreducibly core functions of defence, tax and internal security. The consequential growing assertiveness by the finance sector, the mega-corporations and a 24/7 intrusive media has greatly inhibited the capacity of government to knock heads together, push through compromises between competing interests and enforce the leadership the electorate expects, even to the extent of No. 10 sometimes seeming to be the agent of the real power that has been outsourced elsewhere. To conceal the reality of this mounting defenestration of democratic governance in Britain, a toxic culture of spin and manipulation has been developed to give an impression of power and authority which is actually ebbing away.

It would certainly require great political courage to defy the neo-liberal capitalist model and the Washington consensus, which has dominated the world for the last three decades, though the breaking of this model in the financial crash of 2008–9 and ensuing global economic stagnation clearly provides the opportunity and indeed provokes the necessity. However, the successive weak governments of Blair, Brown and Cameron made the Mephistophelean deal with these forces not even to attempt defiance, but rather to go to endless lengths to placate them. It led to a decade studded with Brown's lyrical paeans to the high priests of finance at the Mansion House, Blair's sycophantic efforts to win over a right-wing press and appease Bush's war presidency, and until recently, to Cameron's behind-the-scenes courting of Murdoch and News International. If Britain is to reverse its present seemingly irrevocable decline, the power models that currently drive its finance, industry, media and politics all need to be radically transformed. Parts 2 and 3 of this book set out how this should be done.

PART 2

WHY NEO-LIBERAL CAPITALISM MUST BE REPLACED

CHAPTER VI

THE ROOT OF THE PROBLEM

All these foregoing fundamental issues – persistent economic decline, the fracturing of social cohesion, over-exploitation of planetary resources and neglect of the climate change threat, the commercial coarsening of society's values, and a seriously dysfunctional power structure – derive from the dynamics of the underlying economic system that produced them, neo-liberal capitalism, sometimes referred to as market fundamentalism. The essential characteristics of this system are the freeing up of markets to operate in as nearly wholly untrammelled a manner as possible, the deregulation of finance, shrinking the state to the minimum role compatible only with security and defence of the realm, privatisation of all industry and services outside this tiny central state core, and empowerment of the private sector as the driving force directing all aspects of economic and financial governance. This chapter explores the performance of this system since it superseded the earlier 'managed' capitalism that prevailed between 1945 and 1980.

(I) THE NEO-LIBERAL RECORD

(i) Growth

Neo-liberalism held the belief that maximising market freedoms was the best way to generate wealth. The post-1980 record, however, reveals a different pattern. After three decades of dereg- ulation and tax cuts for the rich, growth slowed down rather than accelerated in almost all countries. The world economy, which was growing at about 3 per cent a year per capita in the 'bad old days' of widespread regulation and 'punitive' taxation for the rich in the 1960s and 1970s has grown at only about half that rate in the last thirty years. In Britain the average annual per capita income growth in the 1960s and 1970s was 2.4 per cent when the country was allegedly suffering from the 'British disease'. But since 1990, after Thatcher had supposedly cured the country of the disease amid heroic struggles in the 1980s, income growth has fallen to just 1.7 per cent a year.

(ii) Stability

The decade of uninterrupted growth, low and stable inflation, and falling unemployment after 1997 might seem to support the success of underlying neo-liberal doctrines embellished by Brown's rules-based monetary prudence and fiscal 'golden rules'. In fact, the reality was rather different. New Labour inherited a period of steady economic expansion after 1992 brought about by a loosening of monetary policy and a more competitive exchange rate following expulsion from the ERM (Exchange Rate Mechanism). The economy was driven by a consumption- led boom fuelled by house price inflation and readily available credit. The enormous growth of consumption led both to huge levels of debt and insolvency, with disastrous results when the boom broke in 2008–9, and also to persistent structural balance of payments deficits. Even the appearance of achieving the golden rule was managed largely by the huge expansion of the PFI (the Private Finance Initiative), which allowed a big increase in public expenditure while putting the big rise in public liabilities offline. Above all, the decade of growth and prosperity was brought about at the price of an unduly lax monetary policy, regulation-lite markets and neglect of systemic financial risk arising from securitised derivatives and other structured finance, all of which led to the biggest financial bust for a century.

(iii) Wealth

Neo-liberalism has repeatedly been lauded as the greatest generator of wealth the world has ever seen. Again, the record suggests otherwise. It has in fact skewed the allocation of wealth dramatically towards the already rich, particularly ever smaller sub-groups within the top 1 per cent elite, while at the same time squeezing the incomes of the average and poorest citizens. In the UK the share of national income of the bottom tenth almost halved from 4.2 per cent in 1979 to only 2.7 per cent in 2002, and loss of earning power was transformed into high debt. For the population as a whole, while real household income grew over this period (even if more slowly than in the post-war boom, and falling after the early 2000s), household debt quadrupled from 20 per cent of GDP in 1980 to 80 per cent and still rising by 2008.

The impact in the US was even more stark. The income of the poorest fifth of households rose during the age of managed capitalism (1947–73) by 116 per cent, higher than any other quintile, but then under the succeeding era of deregulated market capitalism (1974–2004) it rose by just 2.8 per cent. The real wages of the average US male worker are now lower than in 1979 and for the poorest fifth much lower. But personal debt as a proportion of GDP has more than doubled from 46 per cent in 1979 to

98 per cent in 2008. Thus, so far from spreading wealth neo-liberalism has narrowed it drastically to the top 1–2 per cent at the expense of the vast majority of the rest of the population.

(iv) Competitiveness

It is certainly true that the neo-liberal medicine administered during the Thatcher–Major years secured a strong upturn in labour productivity growth in manufacturing, which virtually doubled from 1.9 per cent a year during 1960–79 to 3.6 per cent a year during 1979–96. This indicates that the government's supply-side measures, together with massive job-shedding during the 1980–82 recession, had most effect where, in manufacturing, UK productivity had fallen back spectacularly relative to leading European countries in the previous thirty years. The momentum of catch-up, however, did not persist into succeeding decades. Indeed, the central test of competitiveness, the country's balance of payments in traded goods, continued to deteriorate until it reached the staggering level of just under £100 billion a year in 2010, equal to 6.8 per cent of GDP. Until 1987 the surplus on financial services covered this deficit, but since then the gap has steadily widened, until by 2010 it covered only half or less. This deterioration in the capacity of the UK to pay its way is simply unsustainable since it depends on foreigners' willingness either to accept UK Treasury bonds or to purchase UK businesses or commercial or other property, and this will not happen indefinitely if perception of UK economic value continues to fall. At that point UK living standards would be forced down significantly.

(v) A balanced economy

Winston Churchill famously remarked in the 1920s that he would rather see finance as the servant of industry than as its master. Free market neo-liberalism, however, has altered the balance of power within capitalist economies overwhelmingly towards finance. Since the 1960s the proportion of total corporate profits represented by the pre-tax profits of the finance sector has nearly tripled from 14 per cent to 39 per cent by 2008. While in the 1980s the total world stock of financial assets was roughly equivalent to world GDP, by 2008 it had reached a level tripling global GDP. This has had serious detrimental consequences both for the international power structure and within the UK in terms of increasing pressure crowding out manufacturing and public and commercial services – a major cause of Britain's relative decline.

By deregulating finance, neo-liberalism enormously increased the power of mobile shareholders to pursue short-term profits and high dividends, and discouraged long-term investments in, for example, machinery and R&D. Shareholders further advanced such detriment by paying astronomical salaries, huge bonuses and lucrative incentive schemes to managers to make cuts for short-term gains even though it weakened the long-run growth prospects of the company – a factor that has seriously damaged UK competitiveness.

(vi) UK interests versus the global market

Neo-liberalism has adopted the dogmatic principle that there should be no intervention in market transactions even if they involve the sale abroad of key UK companies or commercial property which may be integral to the strategic economic interests of the country. The view is taken that the untrammelled market will secure the best long-term interests of the UK. This is, however, a view not taken by any other country, as the evidence already quoted in Chapter V (2) illustrates. If the results of operating this unilateral sacrifice of the national interest could be shown from thirty years of experience to be beneficial to the UK, it would be taken seriously by other countries and probably adopted by them too. But there is no evidence that it has had this beneficial effect. Indeed, it would be surprising if it had, since under neo-liberal capitalism decisions about UK assets are not made to suit the national interest but rather to suit the financial or power interests of large-scale capital.

(vii) Social and environmental standards

The corollary of concentrating on markets as the universal panacea has influences on the wider culture. It has led to the relentless commercialisation of all aspects of human life and an obsessive fixation on individualism to the exclusion of wider social relationships (epitomised by Thatcher's 'there is no such thing as society'). The rise in personal and financial insecurity reflects neo-liberalism's marginalisation of social capital and the widespread decline in voluntary, community and charitable organisations,[36] a process likely to be pushed further by the 2010–15 spending cuts. The marketisation of the public role via wholesale privatisation or the preferential private financing of state functions has diminished social and community life without achieving obvious economic gain, seriously damaging social cohesion.

Equally, the neo-liberal ethic of wealth maximisation at all costs has either ignored or subordinated the overarching imperative to deal with the imminent threat from climate chaos, energy shortage and over-exploitation of global natural resources. These

---

36   Mason, P., 'A Last Chance', *New Statesman*, 10 November 2008.

fundamental issues that threaten human civilisation have been sidelined on the grounds that they are over-costly distractions from the real business of maximising profits, or that they reflect future uncertainties whose cost it is neither necessary nor wise to discount now, or that if there is a problem at all, advances in technology will solve it in due course. This head-in-the-sand attitude represents such an existential threat to human society that it is remarkable that such a narrow, partisan, self-indulgent economic model has prevailed.

(2) BUT DIDN'T MRS THATCHER REVERSE BRITAIN'S ECONOMIC DECLINE?

Despite these huge downsides to neo-liberal capitalism, it is often asserted that at least Thatcher turned around the persisting decline of Britain and that, however painful the costs, it had to be done and the results have justified the means. More than two decades on, it is worth, therefore, seeking an objective assessment of both the policies and their costs.

One key objective was industrial restructuring, not only to secure the big improvements in labour productivity growth already referred to, but to rebalance the economy in favour of finance. It was argued that the monetary discipline of the Medium Term Financial Strategy (MTFS) was industry friendly because it generated a predictable financial strategy to replace stop–go. Deregulation would strengthen industry because the competition for capital would be increased. And privatisation would boost the economy by introducing efficiency criteria into the privatised utilities. In the event the results were rather different. The MTFS tight money regime dismantled a large swathe of manufacturing industry rather than regenerating it. Financial deregulation set off a credit boom and growing access to international finance, which together created high company indebtedness without changing the short-termism of the banks and the markets and their lack of interest in industrial production. And privatisation of the utilities did not bring about the planned improvements in the infrastructure.

Moreover the share of investment in GDP did not rise. OECD comparative figures show the UK, already one of the lowest OECD countries at 14.6 per cent in 1960–73, slipping back slightly further to 13.8 per cent in 1980–89 and then to 13.2 per cent in 1990–95. There may, however, have been some improvement in the quality of investment given the rising proportion due to foreign direct investment (FDI), since recent studies have found that FDI through its impact on technological change probably produced some 30 per cent of labour productivity growth in manufacturing between 1985 and 1995.[37] Investment in human capital increased markedly: real expenditure on training almost trebled 1971–89, the proportion of sixteen-year-olds staying on in full-time education rose from 47 per cent in 1986 to 71 per cent in 1996, the number of vocational qualifications obtained rose 23 per cent to 912,000 during the first half of the 1990s, and the proportion of managers who were graduates more than doubled between 1976 and 1986.[38]

In terms of total factor productivity growth in the business sector, the OECD comparative tables show that the UK moved up from eleventh position (at 2.6 per cent per year) in 1960–73 to fourth (at 1.5 per cent per year) in 1979–95, i.e. UK productivity growth declined, but less fast than in other countries. Several

---

37 Coakley, J. and Harris, L., 'Financial Globalisation and Deregulation', in Michie, J. (ed.), *The Economic Legacy 1979–92*, Academic Press, 1992.

38 Barrell, R. and Pain, N., 'Foreign Direct Investment, Technological Change and Economic Growth within Europe', *Economic Journal*, vol. 107, 1997, pp. 1770–86.

factors influenced this. The replacement ratio (the proportion of previous wages covered by unemployment benefits in the event of redundancy) fell by 20 per cent between 1980 and 1990. The coverage of collective bargaining within the total workforce declined from 70 per cent in 1980 to 47 per cent in 1994. And the trade union differential (the increment in wages produced by trade union bargaining) was reduced following the education and training reforms designed to tackle the unskilled worker problem. Together, these factors were judged sufficient to reduce equilibrium unemployment (NAIRU) by some 4 percentage points. The argument used to support this somewhat specious claim was that, while unemployment reached a post-war high of 3.2 million in August 1986, it would have been higher still without these measures.

The Thatcherite goal of rolling back the frontiers of the state led to mixed results. Overall in real terms state spending did not fall after 1979, but increased. At constant prices it actually rose rapidly after 1978–9 and nearly reached 16 per cent higher by 1986–7. But because of the enormous additional outlay in unemployment and supplementary benefit from the tripling of unemployment, this overall increase served to conceal the depth of the cuts in other areas. In the first three years to 1982, investment by central and local government fell by 40 per cent, half of it in housing, and by 1997 housing's share of GDP had been cut drastically from 6.1 per cent to 1.6 per cent, with annual house-building more than halved.

But Thatcher's neo-liberalism, like any economic system, cannot be judged on its economic record alone without regard to its impacts on society. The corollaries of authoritarian populist capitalism were sharply widening inequality and the replacement of the previous social democratic welfare state with a slimmed-down social security state that was discretionary, means tested and minimalist. A house-owning, pension-owning, share-owning and private medical insurance-holding system subsidised through tax reliefs was promoted as a substitute for council housing, adequate state pensions, income support and a national health service. Where individuals and families could not make adequate private provision, a no-frills state system would be subject to rationing by queuing or based on revolving, cash-limited 'social funds'. Inevitably this regimen led to a tripling of child poverty, a polarisation of living standards, aggravation of regional inequalities, the impoverishing of inner cities, and persisting unemployment – even intergenerational unemployment – in areas laid waste by the decimation of manufacturing industry.

(3) LESSONS ABOUT NEO-LIBERALISM TO BE DRAWN FROM THE THATCHER ERA

While performing the important service of sweeping away the drift, complacency and inefficiency of 1950–70s British industry, Thatcher's programme failed in three key respects. First, she did not address most of the downsides of neo-liberal capitalism outlined in section (1), but rather exacerbated them, indeed championed them. Second, the successes she did achieve redressed some of the shortcomings in economic performance where Britain had fallen badly behind in previous decades, but failed to carry through to succeeding decades. This was not because Thatcher herself was no longer there to drive her programme forward, but rather because the main methods she used – massive redundancies in stripping down companies to meet market competition and closing down old industries wholesale – were once-only remedies which, once exhausted, left the economy exposed to the market but without the back-up support which other countries had to manage it well. And third, a campaign of class war and outright destruction of working-class institutions was hardly a recipe for uniting a country behind agreed, even if painful, objectives in which all sections of the population had a stake and were motivated to make their contribution.

More specifically there are several other important lessons to be drawn from the Thatcher era. First, the idea that was propagated at the centre of the project, that unfettered markets were the answer to everything and that the role of government was to get out of the way, is a caricature of any sensible and balanced economic policy. It reflects the power aspirations of the economic elite, not at all the best interests of the country as a whole. Markets unquestionably have a central role to play, but they require careful supervision. They can readily degenerate into oligopoly or cartels or other anti-competitive measures, they can encourage short-termism at the expense of long-term market share, their cyclical pattern (especially in financial markets) can often overshoot at both peak and nadir, their pattern of capital investment often does not match the national requirement, they cannot alone recover from a downward spiral of recession without a level of economic destruction that is politically intolerable, they can generate a degree of inequality in wealth and power that overrides democratic accountability and political assent, and they give inadequate regard to employment needs as opposed to sales and profits, among other potential deficiencies. The market is not therefore the answer to everything – a lesson that still has to be learnt in the light of Tory ideology (2010–13) targeting all public services for privatisation.

Second, the dominant motif of contemporary neo-liberalism

– that the state should keep out of economic activity and never intervene, that it is no good at picking winners, that it is hopelessly inefficient – is equally misplaced. Of course the state, if that power is mishandled, can become over-dominant and its operations unnecessarily bureaucratic, and it can unwisely reflect the political needs of ministers. But there is a big difference between micro-management and strategic support. There are far more examples (several outlined in Chapter VII) where governments, working alongside and in support of industry, have helped to produce results that industry by itself would not have been able to achieve.

A third lesson to be drawn from the Thatcher era concerns the neo-liberal charge that the private sector exemplifies efficiency and the public sector the reverse. Again this is a mantra for which the evidence is disparate and inconclusive. There are many examples of very high levels of efficiency in both the private and public sectors, as well as numerous examples of crass inefficiency in both. The evidence suggests that the performance outcome is more a reflection on the quality of management than on the public or private status of the organisation. Direct comparisons of productivity between the two sectors are difficult to make because many public services produce various dimensions of output that society values, but which are not readily monetised, and hence the relative valuations of each dimension to construct aggregate measures cannot be gauged in any plausible manner. However, it is instructive that the latest measure of public sector labour productivity by the Office for National Statistics found that in the last quarter of 2011 gross-value-added labour produc-tivity fell by 1.0 per cent in the economy as a whole compared with the first quarter of 2008, but grew over the same period in the government services sector by 2.7 per cent.

(4) A NEW ECONOMIC MODEL TO SUPERSEDE THE DOWNSIDES OF NEO-LIBERALISM

What, then, are the conditions to construct an alternative economic model which seeks to preclude the detrimental consequences of the neo-liberal record as set out, as well as to learn the lessons from the Thatcher era? Perhaps the first, most crucial, requirement is that it should be sustainable in the sense that it arrests the decline of the British economy, which, despite a temporary upturn in the Thatcher years, has continued unabated for a century. That means establishing an economy where the long-term balance of payments is at least broadly stable and preferably positive, where the exchange rate can be maintained at a long-term equilibrium, and where the country in a global market can therefore earn its way to keep and, over time, improve its living standards. At present the failure to do this has been masked by the right opting for a gargantuan rise in private borrowing to maintain unearned consumption, and by the left looking to regular devaluation to bring the country into line with its diminishing competitiveness. Neither is an acceptable or sustainable response to long-term decline, merely addressing the symptoms, not the underlying causes.

The second essential requirement is that the economy operates, and is seen to operate, in the interests of the broad mass of the population, not a minuscule elite. This requires radical action to redress the current excessive inequality in the ownership of wealth, property and land, as well as the establishment and promotion of fundamentally different principles governing remuneration at the extremes of income distribution, at both the bottom and the top. Similarly, the imbalance of power, currently at its most extreme for a century, needs to be greatly reduced if equality of opportunity is to be more than a purely aspirational cipher. Nor is this an ideological quirk. The country will never be able to achieve its potential if the top 1 per cent elite over-whelmingly appropriate the rewards for themselves, social and occupational mobility is largely blocked, and the latent abilities of large sections of the population cannot be realised.

The third objective should be the attainment of full employment as a prime macroeconomic goal in its own right, not the use of unemployment as a residual variable for the control of inflation. Full employment (or as near to it as is feasible) extends economic opportunities as widely as possible, produces a fairer balance of power within industrial relations, reduces inequality and poverty, diminishes alienation and the development of an antagonistic underclass culture, and hugely enhances social cohesion and community vitality. To maintain employment at high levels, demand management measures have a role in controlling inflationary pressures, but the main driver in maintaining equilibrium should lie in enhancing competitiveness across the board.

That will not be secured by monetarist deflationary policies which have been tried so often in the past, whether via Milton Friedman's 'natural' rate of unemployment, which he developed from Fisher's quantity theory of money; Thatcher's constant weakening of labour terms and conditions; or Osborne's oxymoronic expansionary fiscal contraction. It will only be achieved by positive supply-side measures designed to increase manufacturing skills, ensure adequate industrial funding, enhance both the level and quality of R&D, restore broken supply chains and incentivise increasing long-term market share over short-term profiteering. Equally, in a recessionary cycle stability should be restored not by fiscal contraction leading to prolonged austerity but by public sector capital investment (e.g. in infrastructure and house-building) to halt the downturn and provide enough stimulus to growth and job creation and thus to aggregate demand in order to encourage the revival of private investment as the basis of a sustained upturn.

The fourth requirement is a major rebalancing of the economy from finance to industry. The City of London is currently twice as large, as a proportion of the total economy, as the financial centres of Germany, France and other main European countries, while UK manufacturing has shrunk drastically from 26 per cent of total output to just 11 per cent by 2009, a far steeper drop than in the main competitor countries. That imbalance has to be urgently corrected since services cannot alone maintain the UK standard of living.

The fifth requirement is a redrawing of the respective roles of the state and the markets. In the post-war 'managed' capitalism of 1948–73 the nationalised industries and centralised planning played a major part, while in the following period of neo-liberal capitalism, 1980–2007, the markets, particularly in finance, were almost entirely deregulated and both public industries and services very largely privatised. Both of these ideological positions involved a mutual antagonism between the public and private sectors and both were found to involve serious deficiencies. By contrast, a new settlement is needed which seeks to optimise the interactive roles of each. Markets should be incentivised to enhance their innovative and entrepreneurial capacities, but need supervision by the state for such key functions as maintaining free entry, preventing commercial abuses, strengthening competitiveness, ensuring adequate funding flows and filling gaps or remedying failures left by the private sector.

The state has a duty to oversee and foster the overall operation of the economy and its component parts, including regulating economic cycles, holding the ring between conflicting interests, and promoting the economic rights of all citizens, but to do so in a way that works as compatibly as possible with the operation of markets.

The sixth key requirement of a new economic model to supersede the failures of neo-liberal capitalism is the securing of a broad balance between the economic, social and environmental goals of the nation. Deregulated markets have concentrated almost exclusively on maximising wealth to the exclusion of social and community values, labour rights and protections, and environmental and climate imperatives. Educational, geographical and financial inequalities have flourished, employment rights at work have been restricted and protective legislation diminished, and measures to advance a 'green' economy and reverse the serious threat of catastrophic climate change have been largely sidelined. Counter-balancing these trends and securing a better mix between these wider objectives, all important in their own right, requires a very different model from one driven by self-regulation by economic elites, and the rest of Part 3 explores how that alternative model might work.

CHAPTER VII

ALTERNATIVES TO THE CURRENT UK CAPITALIST MODEL

(I) THE US POLITICAL ECONOMY

Not all of the world's capitalist systems have developed in the manner of Anglo-Saxon financialisation. This model reached its apogee in the extreme individualistic and libertarian form of American capitalism.[39] Its dominant financial system is driven by the Wall Street markets demanding very high rewards which in turn require high efficiency in product markets and high flexibility of labour markets, with unfettered ease for employers to hire and fire. Job creation is strong, but unions are weak, employment regulation is very limited and job turnover is high to suit the vagaries of market demand. Both company taxation and individual taxation are low by international standards and social security contributions are also low, leading to low and means-tested welfare benefits. Moreover workers' wages remain very depressed, with the bottom tenth of the workforce paid only some one-third of median earnings compared with the European average of two-thirds, and have stagnated at that level since the early 1970s. This overall framework has led to extremes, with many US universities achieving world-beating successes

---

39   Hutton, W., *The State We're In*, Vintage, 1996, p. 258.

while education for the poor remains distinctly low-standard, with notable skills qualifications at the middle–top ranges of the workforce combined with widespread inadequate literacy at the bottom end, and with yawning inequality between Croesus-like wealth at the top and stark deprivation at the bottom.

Because companies are at constant risk of being taken over by predatory buying of their shares on the stock market if their share price drops, there is enormous pressure to maintain the growth of short-term profits and dividend payments at all costs – one key reason why US industry has been steadily hollowed out. There is no commitment to suppliers other than the lowest bidder in regularly tendered contracts, nor to essential social goals, which are externalised to be prosecuted by federal or state regulators. Many of these institutional protections, however, have been gradually whittled away over time. The long-term investment credit bank developed by Roosevelt, the Reconstruction Finance Corporation, was abolished in the 1950s. The state-run bodies set up to run housing finance, Freddie Mac and Fannie Mae, were later privatised but then had to be rescued from collapse in 2008. The Glass–Steagall Act of the 1930s, which required the banks to separate high-street banking from securities speculation, was repealed in 1996, heralding the meltdown a decade later.

Nevertheless intervention at federal level has provided significant support for US industry in R&D, funding and trade protection. Federal R&D expenditure focused particularly on defence gave an important stimulus to the high-tech industry. The space programme provided crucial spin-offs for the electronics industry, while the Pentagon-driven military–industrial complex hugely boosted the US semiconductor industry. Despite the emphasis on free markets, the Buy America Act ensured that public procurement favours US suppliers, and the 'super 301' trade legislation enabled the US government to retaliate unilaterally against countries perceived to be unfairly blocking US exports or subsidising their own exports.

British finance capitalism demands the same high returns from companies and equally displays the same lack of commitment to wider social goals as the US. But the UK statutory regulation is more limited – notoriously 'light touch' – and there are no strong regional or state banks to intermediate this pressure on small businesses and employees. The UK labour market exhibits the same downsides of high turnover and high income inequality, but without the partial compensation of greater US mobility and more marked US managerial dynamism. Nor does the UK have either the protective cover provided by the co-operative and community-based structures of Asian capitalism or any equivalent of the German *Mittelstand* for middle-sized companies.

(2) THE EU SOCIAL MARKET

By comparison with the US–UK model, the European social market ideal has developed a very different variety of capitalism. As Will Hutton has shown in his perceptive analysis of the different systems, there are markedly less adversarial overtones. It is based on capital–labour partnership, greater bank commitment to the companies funded, a more comprehensive and inclusive welfare system, and a much higher degree of formal power-sharing in its politics. This framework, while still resonating to market signals, is much more geared to co-operation, investment and high productivity. By the same token, however, accommodation to adverse economic conditions is slower because decision-making is more shared and diffuse and regulatory mechanisms can also prevent rapid responses.

The social market is strongly imbued with the sense of social cohesion. In Germany the capital–market partnership inspires co-decision-making (*mitbestimmung*) in both the boardroom and works council, whereby unions agree not to use the strike weapon or to pursue their self-interest without regard to the company's problems in return for the bosses forgoing the managerial right to rule and commitment to engage in genuine consultation. Both capital and labour are represented by wide-ranging self-governing organisations which manage both wages and industrial relations with a greater sense of mutuality of inter-est, so that labour turnover rates are lower than in the US and wages much higher. This system is supported, crucially, by the banks, which sit on the company boards, engage closely as long-term shareholders and stay loyal so that contested takeovers (the adversarial centrepiece of Anglo-Saxon capitalism) are almost unheard of.

The system is buttressed by a mutually reinforcing web of political, economic and social interconnected institutions exhib-iting a similar philosophy. The welfare network (*Sozialstaat*) expresses social solidarity through a high level of social protec-tion. The dual vocational system linking academic education with industrial experience produces a constant flow of trained apprentices underpinning the high levels of German productiv-ity. More than twice the proportion of German employees are technically qualified compared with British employees, and craft skills figure strongly in German culture. Again, in a market system based more on co-operation than confrontation strong unions on works councils and supervisory boards are powerful agents of industrial restructuring, pushing through job cuts and wage reductions negotiated towards long-term goals.

Similarly, by contrast with Britain, where the governing party controls the state machine exclusively, under Rhine-Alpine social market arrangements a PR voting system ensures a stronger sense of a common public interest in which power-sharing is regularised. Regional government is entrenched and firmly independent, and the state is seen rather as a component of civil society than as the over-dominant player. Because public agencies act as social partners obliged to consider wider interests, they act as agents in building consensus. Typically the Bundesbank, composed of the presidents of the regional state banks appointed by the regional governments, reflects political opinion across the spectrum, which allows a consensus more easily to develop in monetary policy.

Again, unlike US–UK emphasis on unrestrained globalisation, Germany's institutional framework offers some protection against unfettered market forces. The family-owned medium-sized business sector (*Mittelstand*) has the benefit of long-term funding from the regional state banks, it enjoys the advantage of reliable contracts with larger companies committed to co-operative relationships, and it gains from clustering in cities and regions which have the autonomy to shape their industrial policy to suit its needs.

The model is not, however, without significant internal strains. Globalisation and cost competition have forced the *Mittelstand* to import supplies from low-cost countries abroad and forced the banks to succumb to more short-term pressures. 'Lean production', sub-contracting and 'just in time' deliveries to save on inventories are increasingly required to take on competition from Japan and low-wage developing countries, though more in the form of updating the model rather than replacing it – through improved training, better technology transfer and new networks to disseminate market data. Even so, trade unions can vigorously oppose outsourcing, the *Sozialstaat* interlocking network of institutions is costly, and the bank–industry relationship can become incestuous and corrupt.

(3) EAST ASIAN CAPITALISM

The third capitalist genre is the east Asian version, which, while being intensely competitive, takes further still the co-operative instincts of the European social market. Its underlying principles emphasise long-term relationships, even more than in the EU model, as the basis for wealth creation and productivity. Since the dominant factor of production is seen to be labour, the value system stresses trust, reputation and continuity, though that doesn't prevent pay and working conditions from often being poor and well below Western levels. At least until the Japanese property crash and ensuing stagnation from the early 1990s, the regulated banking system was the least market mediated and the most customer committed of the three capitalist variants. That secure financial backing allowed Japanese companies to achieve breakthroughs with their workforce and suppliers beyond the reach of price-driven Western firms. These shop floor efficiencies then laid the foundations for a virtuous spiral of growth, increased investment, rising productivity and attention to constant quality improvement.

The principle of consensus is dominant, even more than in the EU version. So far from being commodities of production, the residual variable in Western market theory, employees see themselves as belonging to their firm as their core social unit. The implicit contract is that the firm offers lifetime employment, social support and a pension for retirement in return for loyalty and commitment. Inequality is low, there is a strong sense of common purpose in achieving a highly competitive production culture, and the state acts as promoter of a consensus and then guides firms and banks to fulfil it. The emphasis on inclusiveness, tolerance and harmony can still be anchored firmly on business success, but the permeability between Japanese government, society and business can undermine clarity of role, weaken accountability and lead to widespread corruption. Nevertheless the influence exerted by MITI (the Ministry of International Trade and Industry) in industrial restructuring and co-ordinating company strategies was dominant for several decades, though its dirigisme in the recent period has been reduced both by the paralysis in the political system and by the prolonged recession.

As with the US market and German social-state systems, the various elements of the east Asian model interlock and are mutually reinforcing. The finance commitment enables the parallel commitment to workers and supplier, which itself then delivers the productivity gains to justify the financial commitment being made. Thus economic competitiveness is generated without being mediated through the ruthlessness of impersonal price signals in the pure market system. The big city banks act as the hub of dense corporate cross-shareholdings, dispensing long-term loans, presiding over joint venture negotiations and, where necessary, restructuring companies in distress.

What is the more remarkable is that this east Asian system of government and business by consent – the antithesis of Western

notions of parliamentary sovereignty and top-down governance –
is of relatively recent origin. Between the First and Second World
Wars the Japanese economy functioned on very similar capitalist
lines to the West, with strong emphasis on immediate profits,
short-term loans, bonus and share option schemes for managers,
and a flexible labour market which hired and fired workers as
the economic cycle required. Significantly the perceived degen-
eration of management and the greed and selfishness of the
big shareholders propelled a strong reaction which pushed
the Japanese government in the 1930s into a fundamental reshaping of the finance and labour system along lines which flowered so
dramatically from the 1960s. Shareholder rights were restricted,
dividends limited, workers' committees were given the role of
boosting production and banks were tasked with making investment loans in the national interest rather than simply geared to
short-term private profit. Given the extraordinary success of this
policy, the relevance of this transformation can hardly be lost on
the West of the 2010s, and particularly on the UK.

The moral of this is that the development of this much more
personalised and relational capitalism didn't evolve organically.
It was thrown up by powerful underlying social and economic
forces – repudiation of a failing, greedy system, a national drive
to catch up with the West, and a readiness to explore with experiments of what might work better. The contrast with the UK is
stark: Britain has never been forced to change by defeat in war,
its class system is deeply embedded in immobility, and there is
no sense in the elite of any fundamental need to change.

(4) THE RISE OF STATE CAPITALISM IN THE EMERGING WORLD

The most powerful and persistent challenge, however, to Western neo-liberal capitalism comes from the rise of state capitalism in emerging economies. State-directed capitalism is not new – indeed it goes back to the East India Company in the seventeenth century. But it is undergoing a remarkable revival. The world's ten biggest oil-and-gas firms, measured by reserves, are all state owned, and state-owned enterprises (SOEs) account for 80 per cent of the value of China's stock market and 62 per cent of Russia's. SOEs account for twenty-eight of the emerging world's 100 biggest companies, and some of them are truly colossal giants – China Mobile, for example, has 600 million customers. SOEs also accounted for a third of the emerging world's foreign direct investment in 2003–10. Even in the developed world a version of the state capitalist brand has flourished. Despite the Western drive for privatisation and deregulation since the 1980s, the rich world still contains many state-owned or state-dominated companies, including France owning 85 per cent of EDF, Japan 50 per cent of Japan Tobacco, and Germany 32 per cent of Deutsche Telekom. Across the OECD, state-owned companies have a combined value of nearly $2 trillion and employ six million people. However, the state capitalist model remains primarily an Asian and emerging markets phenomenon.

Brazil privatised in the 1990s, but is now pursuing inter-ventionist policies in big companies like Petrobras and the mining giant Vale, and forcing smaller companies to combine to form national champions.[40] South Africa is openly consider-ing nationalising companies and creating national champions. The earliest modern proponent of this approach was Singapore under Lee Kuan Yew, who welcomed foreign firms and accepted

---

40   *The Economist*, 21 January 2012 has a comprehensive special report on the whole new phenomenon of SOEs.

Western management techniques but kept hold of large parts of big companies. Nor is this policy protectionist: the best national champions are outward-looking, win contracts abroad and take over foreign companies. Indeed, they are flourishing in the emerging world's dynamic markets, where growth has averaged 5.5 per cent a year compared with the rich world's 1.6 per cent over the past few years. And by 2020 they are likely to account for half the world's GDP.

This policy is very different from previous across-the-board nationalisations. In fact the state-owned sector as a whole has been hugely reduced, now making up only a third of China's and Russia's GDP, compared with almost all only two decades ago. What has happened, though, is not liberalisation, but selective pruning in which governments have let go small companies but strengthened their grip on the largest. Paradoxically, therefore, the SOEs have become wealthier and more powerful even though the overall state sector is shrinking, and governments have tightened their control over the commanding heights of the economy even though the private sector is growing. As a result, economic power has become increasingly concentrated within an inner group of SOEs. China's 121 largest SOEs increased their total assets eight-fold from $360 billion in 2002 to $2.9 trillion in 2010 (even while their share of GDP declined). Significantly it has been these huge SOEs that were boosted most by state action after the 2007–8 financial crash: in 2009 SOEs received 85 per cent of the $1.4 trillion in bank loans.

Government ownership has also become more sophisticated. Most SOEs hardly report directly to government ministries any longer since most governments now exercise control through share ownership, which is sometimes as low as 10 per cent. Thus in Russia the state has kept golden shares in 181 firms. Total control, with 100 per cent state-owned shares as in Malaysia's Petronas, China's Ocean Shipping Company or Russia's United Aircraft Corporation, is increasingly rare. In addition SOEs have become more productive, with China claiming an increase in return on assets from 0.7 per cent in 1998 to 6.3 per cent in 2006. And among the thirteen national oil companies that control over three-quarters of global oil supplies they are generally well managed, such as Petronas and particularly Saudi Arabia's Aramco (though with exceptions like Petróleos de Venezuela and Mexico's Pemex). Furthermore a new genre has emerged in which national champions are in a formal sense privately owned but receive huge overt or covert support from government, whether that patronage is offered at arm's length because the authorities lack experience of that sector (e.g. IT) or where a private company has become a clear winner. The list of such private–public national champions is long, and in China includes Geely cars, Huawei telecoms equipment and Haier white goods.

Another important offshoot of this developing economic force is their assemblage of vast pools of capital as sovereign wealth funds. Begun by Singapore in 1953, expanded by the petro-states in the 1970s, the trend has most recently accelerated as a result of the surge in energy prices, even before growth has fully recovered after the crash, and the colossal current account surplus accumulated by China. Total global sovereign wealth funds already control $4.8 trillion in assets, expected to reach $10 trillion by 2020, and include Abu Dhabi Investment Authority's $627 billion, the Saudi SAMA foreign holdings company's $473 billion and China's SAFE Investment

Company with $568 billion and again China's Investment
Corporation with $410 billion. One effect of this will be to
compel the global finance system to move from a London–New
York-centred model to a network with many intersecting and
interconnected centres which prefer to do business directly with
each other rather than via rich-world intermediaries.

The degree of state control over companies varies considerably.
In China the Communist Party has cells in most big companies,
private as well as state owned, which appoint top managers,
shadow formal board meetings and often overturn their decisions,
as well as working with management to regulate workers' pay. Its
Organisation Department wields colossal power in appointing
all the top figures in Chinese industry (e.g. in reshuffling the
heads of the three biggest telecoms companies in 2004, rotating
the chiefs of the three biggest airlines in 2009, and then of the
three biggest oil companies in 2010), thus ensuring that loyalty
to the party remains paramount. The party-state encourages
industry clusters by offering preferential access to contracts and
stock market listings. But power is exercised through the State-
Owned Assets Supervision and Administration Commission,
owning 100 per cent of the shares in holding companies, which
in turn own lesser, but still majority, shares in their divisions.

Russian capitalism presents a different model, dominated by a
few gigantic firms controlled by a cabal of security officials. After
the wild privatisations of the Yeltsin era, dispersed companies
have been rejoined into national champions including Aeroflot
and Russian Technologies or renationalised like the oil company
Rosneft, which took back most of Khodorkovsky's Yukos
empire, and Gazprom, which bought Sibneft from Abramovich.
In addition, the state has huge shareholdings in the biggest

and most strategic companies, including Transneft (pipelines), Sukhoi (aircraft), Sberbank (banking) and Unified Energy Systems (electricity). The private sector oligarchs have been subdued – brutally in the case of Khodorkovsky, as a warning to others – and replaced by state oligarchs, most of them ex-KGB officials with close ties to Putin. This Russia, Inc. controls the country's most lucrative assets: oil and gas, nuclear power, arms, metals, diamonds, aviation and transport. At the same time it has been active in the global market, with oil and gas companies buying similar firms abroad, Rosneft raising $11 billion on the London stock exchange, and Russia's sovereign wealth funds on a buying spree of foreign companies.

Another, more subtle, form of state capitalism comes from Brazil, which in the 1980s had more than 500 SOEs but which over the next decade deployed widespread privatisation in the face of hyper-inflation, rising deficits and growing sclerosis. This has, however, recently been reversed by the consolidation of a few national champions, especially in natural resources and tele-coms. At the same time, direct government ownership has been replaced by indirect ownership through the Brazilian National Development Bank and its investment subsidiary. By 2009 the latter's holdings were only 4 per cent of the stock market, yet because of the broad spread of minority shareholdings the government exercised great influence over the corporate sector. However, the government has also brought about some national champions by forced mergers of unlikely partners.

There are several conclusions to be drawn from this overall picture of state capitalism. Politicians certainly exert more power over the economy than under liberal capitalism, but it is not all one way: SOEs also wield considerable influence over their supposed political masters. SOEs are also producing a more sophisticated genre of managers, often with a world-class business education and with work experience abroad. Symbiosis between government and the corporate domain is striking: seventeen Chinese political leaders, for example, have come from senior SOE posts, and twenty-seven business leaders serve on the party's Central Committee. SOEs' biggest achievements have been in infrastructure – huge dams, extensive high-speed rail, mobile phone networks and information superhighways, and solar panels. They excel as national champions: two-thirds of emerging-world companies in Fortune 500 are SOEs, and they succeed as the corporate world's ablest learning machines. And state-capitalist countries strongly promote independent innovation: Beijing's Zhongguancun science park houses 20,000 high-tech enterprises, Moscow's Skolkovo high-tech park/enterprise zone is a magnet for indigenous technologists as well as foreign multinationals, and Dubai boasts a knowledge village, an IT corridor and a huge finance centre. But state capitalism has also been at the heart of outward activity, with China's SOEs funding four-fifths of foreign direct investment, in particular tying foreign aid to commercial advantage, notably oil for infrastructure.

The great claim of the axis of state capitalism – China, Russia and the Middle East – is that it has a format which can combine economic dynamism with civic order, exhibiting the best of capitalism without unleashing the chaos that devastated Russia in the 1990s and nearly consumed the US in 2008–9. However, while state capitalism displays lesser volatility and instability than deregulated free markets, that security can come at the price of lower productivity. A 2005 OECD paper found that total factor productivity of private companies was twice that of state companies, and a McKinsey study concluded that companies where the state had a minority stake were on average 70 per cent more productive than SOEs. Nevertheless that has not stopped fears in the West that the rise of state capitalism may undermine the post-war trading system, partly because Western companies are forced to hand over intellectual capital to get access to Chinese markets, but mainly because China's capacity to make vast strategic investments, even creating entire new industries, discriminates decisively against private competitors.

A NEW BUSINESS MODEL: STRATEGY FOR BRITAIN'S RENAISSANCE

CHAPTER VIII

HANDLING THE DEFICIT

Chapter VII has shown that capitalism is not a single entity, but rather has several different varieties, from some of which Britain has important lessons to learn. Chapter VI argued that the UK brand is largely broken and particularly in the last three decades has not promoted the national interest but rather that of a small economic elite. It has also indicated that it is not sustainable in terms of either its overdependence on debt-fuelled demand or its growing failure to pay its way in the world, demonstrated by a yawning balance of payments gap. Part 3 of this book sets out the conditions for achieving growth that is genuinely sustainable. In the immediate term this means turning round the deficit in a manner which does not cause prolonged decline and serious irrecoverable loss to the economy. This is the subject of this chapter. In the medium term, sustainability requires fundamental economic restructuring which redresses the profound flaws and weaknesses which have steadily dragged down the UK economy in recent decades – and indeed, in many respects, since the Second World War. That is the subject of Chapters IX and X. But there is a third dimension of sustainability, namely the long-term accommodation of the global economy within the ecological constraints of the earth. This is discussed in Chapter XVIII.

(I) THE REAL CAUSES OF THE BUDGET DEFICIT

Unsurprisingly since Britain has been dominated since the 1980s by a tiny economic elite of the 1 per cent top earners, when the crash came in 2008–9 it was interpreted by this elite and their messengers in the media in a manner which sought to protect their own interests and to divert the coming pain on to others. Thus Osborne throughout 2010–11 constantly maintained that national debt was out of control because of gross government overspending and therefore public expenditure had to be drastically cut. However, the UK's budget deficit was only 3 per cent in 2007, and it rose to a peak of 11.6 per cent in 2009–10 only because of the £68 billion spent on the bank bail-outs plus a further £850 billion extended for loan guarantees, liquidity schemes and asset protection provision for the banks. Even by mid-2010 UK national debt had only risen to 77 per cent of GDP compared to 75 per cent in Germany, 84 per cent in France, and 93 per cent in the US. Even more significantly, between 1920 and 1960 the UK debt to GDP ratio never fell below 100 per cent and after the Second World War actually reached 250 per cent. In fact the financial crisis was not caused by public sector borrowing at all, but rather by private sector indebtedness on a grand scale. It was not the state that crowded out private enterprise in the preceding years but rather householders' and corporations' ability to borrow too cheaply. As to government borrowing, until 2007 Labour's annual spend did not exceed the Thatcher government's lowest annual spend in eight of her eleven years, and it only rose after 2007 because of the bank bail-outs and the recession they caused.

The real causes that lay behind the sharply rising budget deficit went much deeper than the conventional wisdom of the time. The key New Labour agenda had been to allow the City through the lightest-touch regulation to attract international business on an unprecedented scale and thus to make huge fortunes from which the tax revenues could be creamed off to fund higher public spending and tax credits. But while the bubble in the financial sector grew ever bigger, the manufacturing sector struggled as inflationary pressures were suppressed by cheap goods from emerging economies, notably China. Production moved east while hot money flowed in the opposite direction into the deregulated financial markets of London and New York. The capital flows pushed up the value of sterling, making imports cheaper and exports dearer. Domestic price pressures then required the Bank of England, with its tight remit to control inflation, to cut interest rates, encouraging excessive borrowing, an explosion in debt and higher asset prices.

The ensuing recession once the financial bubble burst was driven by the slump in investment (gross fixed capital formation). Actual GDP peaked at £1.4 trillion (annualised) in the first quarter of 2008, but then fell by £81 billion over the next two years, of which three-quarters was accounted for by the decline in investment and in inventories. The severity of the downturn led to a dramatic fall in tax revenues. From 1997 tax revenues grew at an average rate of 5.6 per cent a year, and on this trend without a recession the tax take would have reached £612 billion in 2009–10, compared to the actual Treasury figure of £498 billion. This shortfall of £114 billion represented three-quarters of the entire budget deficit of £155 billion.

(2) THE QUIXOTIC PARADOX OF 'EXPANSIONARY FISCAL CONTRACTION'

Osborne, however, with the incoming government's agenda to shrink the state, privatise all public services and minimise

welfare, seized the opportunity to turn the crisis to his ideological advantage and laid the foundations for his drastic remedy of
'expansionary fiscal contraction'. The rationale for this counter-
intuitive idea was that wiping out the entire budget deficit of
£155 billion within a very short five-year timescale would make
the economy recover faster and more vigorously from the recession because of the favourable effects of fiscal consolidation on
the bond markets and on expectations in the private sector. As it
happens, there are three relevant British precedents which offer
some test for these theories.

The first was the wielding of the 'Geddes axe' in 1921–2, carried
out by an earlier Tory–Liberal coalition government. Borrowing
for the First World War had sharply increased government debt,
which peaked at 135 per cent of GDP in 1919 (compared with
the expectation today that debt will peak at about 90 per cent in
2015). Under pressure from the Anti-Waste League (opposed
to 'wasteful' government expenditure, founded by Rothermere),
the Geddes Committee of businessmen was commissioned to
produce savings of £100 million on top of the £75 million cuts
already made by the Treasury. As a result government current
spending was cut by a sum equal to about £100 billion at today's
prices (slightly less than today's projected cuts), including sums
crucial for long-term growth like secondary education for poorer
children. Monetary policy was not eased to offset fiscal contraction, under the ill-advised folly of keeping interest rates high to
enable the pound to regain pre-war parity with the dollar. The
result was eight years of exceptionally feeble growth, punctuated
by the 1926 general strike, with the unemployment of insured
workers never falling below 10 per cent (Keynes's 'underemploy-
ment equilibrium'). Furthermore, and significantly for today, the

shrinkage of the economy brought about in 1921–2 caused the national debt actually to grow from 135 per cent in 1919 to 180 per cent in 1923, and it was still higher in 1929 than at the end of the war.

The second relevant precedent was the setting up of the May businessmen's committee in 1931, after the Wall Street crash of 1929 had collapsed global demand and caused unemployment to reach almost 20 per cent, to review the solvency of the Labour government's finances. May projected a budget deficit of £120 million for 1932–3 and demanded £96 million cuts, mostly from benefits and wages, with just £24 million of extra taxes (very similar to Osborne's 77–23 per cent allocation today). The gap in the government's budget was about 10 per cent of projected public spending, again, much the same as today. May's measures, however, failed to restore confidence, and Keynes noted at the time that the May cuts would raise unemployment by 400,000, lower tax revenues and reduce the budget deficit by only £50 million. However, in September 1931, a month after they were imposed, the May Committee and the national coalition government that implemented the cuts were saved from themselves by a mutiny of naval ratings at Invergordon facing a pay cut, and Britain was forced off the gold standard. Paradoxically it was this (unintended) event, rather than any expansionary fiscal contraction, which then delivered four years of solid growth from 1933 to 1937 by enabling interest rates to fall to 2 per cent for the rest of the 1930s and by allowing the pound to devalue by 30 per cent, which boosted exports for eighteen months until the US devalued too.

The third relevant British precedent is Geoffrey Howe's 1981 Budget, which, in order to reduce inflation, took £4 billion or 2 per cent out of the economy at a time when unemployment

was rising. The economy, however, quickly emerged from recession and grew at a brisk pace averaging 3.3 per cent for the next
five years, with inflation dropping in the first two years from
18 per cent to 4 per cent. This might well seem to bear out the
expansionary fiscal contraction theory. However, even the strongest advocates (e.g. the monetarist economist Professor Tim
Congdon) acknowledged that the expansion had much more to
do with the accompanying monetary easing of interest rates and
the restrictions loosened on bank lending, together with a steady
reflation of the world economy and thus of global demand by US
expansionary domestic policies. None of these options, however,
are available in 2010–12 when interest rates have already been
reduced – at 0.5 per cent, almost to the floor – £375 billion of
quantitative easing has still not provided the necessary stimulus, and all restrictions on bank lending have long since been
removed (by the Tories themselves).

It is clear, therefore, that none of these precedents validate
the expansionary fiscal contraction thesis – quite the reverse.
As Skidelsky powerfully argues,[41] the fiscal contraction never
produced economic growth strong enough to replace the output
lost in the preceding slump. It therefore also failed to reduce
the national debt, which rises at times of stagnation and only
reduces at times of growth. It is also highly significant that each
of these historical episodes of very sharp cutbacks generated huge
political unrest – the Invergordon mutiny, the general strike, the
hunger marches of the 1930s, and the miners' strike of 1984–5.
The lesson is that, when recovery did occur, it was cheap money
rather than fiscal contraction that produced it.

41   Skidelsky, R., *Keynes: The Return of the Master*, Penguin 2010.

Osborne does indeed also rely on quantitative easing (printing money), but it has never brought about complete recovery on past occasions since it acts primarily on long-term interest rates rather than aggregate demand. Indeed, its greatest influence is on asset prices, thus prompting another housing boom fuelled by cheap credit, which might seem perverse after three house price bubbles burst disastrously in the last forty years. Above all, since most investment is more sensitive to the level of demand rather than the cost of capital, even very low interest rates might have little effect on economic activity. And the whole question of deficiency of aggregate demand remains unresolved, indeed largely still unrecognised. Keynes's conclusion in 1932 was that if investors (bankers with shattered confidence) demand interest rates which enterprises cannot expect to earn, 'there will be no escape from prolonged and perhaps interminable depression except by direct state intervention to promote and subsidise new investment'. That judgement on neo-liberalism and its associated doctrine designed to contain its excesses could hardly be more appropriate today.

(3) STIMULUS, NOT AUSTERITY

The alternative policy is not to cut the deficit by drastically reducing public spending but to grow the economy by public investment, and thus by substantially cutting unemployment and the payment of benefits (the 'automatic stabilisers') and by increasing tax receipts (from income tax, national insurance contributions, and VAT payments), to raise Exchequer revenues from higher growth. But the obvious riposte to this is: how is the higher public spending to be funded without causing the bond markets to take fright and push up interest rates, making the funding of the country's debt markedly more expensive?

One answer is that to borrow more to increase *consumption* would certainly, and rightly, draw down the wrath of the markets. But modest borrowing (at the current 0.5 per cent interest rate, £30 billion could be borrowed at the knock-down cost of £150 million) which expanded output and thus raised tax revenues would certainly not be ruled out by the financial markets when what they are demanding is a plausible plan which can stabilise the public finances at an acceptable level. Significantly, an IMF study published in September 2010 concluded, in the words of the *FT*, 'that the US and UK could probably increase their public debt burden by another 50 per cent of GDP beyond projected 2015 levels without triggering a crisis'.

Another answer is that there are several untapped sources of funding. These could include: a financial transactions tax (£30 billion) or a scaled-down debit transaction tax (£4.2 billion), a cap on tax relief (£10 billion) or minimum tax rates for the highest earners (£14.9 billion), a general anti-avoidance principle (uncertain, but it could certainly exceed £10 billion), an empty property tax (£5 billion), abolishing the non-domicile rule (£3 billion), higher council tax rates for the most expensive properties (£1.7 billion), removing the ceiling on national insurance contributions (£9.1 billion), ending pension tax reliefs at the higher rate (£14 billion), the restoration of the 50 per cent income tax rate on earnings over £150,000 (£3 billion), increasing HMRC tax inspectors – which this government is cutting from 70,000 to 56,000 by 2014, even though each inspector raises in revenue on average sixty times his salary – in order to cut tax avoidance/evasion by some £10 billion, as well as other options like introducing a land value tax and/or a wealth tax. Collectively these measures could certainly raise a total of between £60 billion and £80 billion a year.

An even fairer way of redistributing the burden would be to concentrate the extra tax take on the ultra-rich alone, the wealthiest segments within the richest 1 per cent. The latest *Sunday Times* Rich List (a sort of *X Factor* for capitalists) records that the wealth of the richest 1,000 in the country (just 0.003 per cent of the total population) more than quadrupled from £99 billion in 1997 to £413 billion in 2008. Even after the bust in 2009 their wealth shot back up again to £414 billion by 2012, an increase of no less than £155 billion in the last three years of austerity[42] – an amount significantly greater than the entire UK budget deficit in that year. Within this group there are now seventy-seven billionaires commanding an ever larger share of the cake: their wealth is now valued at about £269 billion.

If this asset gain of £155 billion accruing to just 1,000 persons (let alone the other 300,000 persons in the richest 1 per cent) were taxed at the current capital gains tax rate of 28 per cent, it would yield £43 billion. That is more than enough to fund an increase in public investment sufficient to create 1–1.5 million jobs over the next two to three years. That expenditure, which would involve no increase in public borrowing at all, would generate the turnaround in the economy so urgently needed, inaugurate an upward growth spiral and rapidly pay for itself in increased tax revenues. The stimulus could be focused on house-building (currently at the lowest rate since 1923 despite the 1.8 million households on council waiting lists), improving transport infrastructure and energy supply, and developing the new green digital economy. And it would uniquely provide the jump-start

---

42 The 24th annual *Sunday Times* survey of Britain's rich, compiled by Philip Beresford, May 2012.

to enable the private sector to begin its long-term revival and unlock the colossal stockpile of cash and bank deposits held by the corporate sector, with UK banks' amounting to £750 billion in 2012. So why won't Osborne do this? Partly because no Tory government will countenance any serious taxation of the very rich, partly because the loss of face for Osborne would be enormous and perhaps career-destroying, but mainly because the hidden Tory agenda has always been the dissolution of the welfare state and the shrinking of the public sector to no more than the security apparatus.

Whatever the motives, this must rank as one the biggest macro-economic policy errors of the last century. The only other errors of comparable magnitude were the restoration of the pound's pre-war dollar parity with the dollar by Churchill in 1924, the brief adoption of monetarist targeting in the early 1980s, which led to sharp and uncontrolled deflation, and the decision in 1990 to enter the European Exchange Rate Mechanism at an over-valued rate of 2.95 Deutschmarks to the pound. All four major errors were made by Conservative Chancellors and caused big increases in unemployment that were unnecessary, and all were based on simplistic macroeconomics. In the 1920s it was the idea that savage domestic cost-cutting could restore the capacity to reach a new higher arbitrary level of financial competitiveness. In 1980 it was that there is a simple and reliable link between some measure of money and inflation. In 1990 it was that the medium-term equilibrium real exchange rate is always equal to the rate of purchasing power parity. And in 2010 it was that private sector demand would automatically replace public sector demand or even that monetary policy in the form of inflation-targeting is always capable of stabilising demand.

(4) THE LONG-TERM PROBLEM OF GENERATING ADEQUATE DEMAND

Even when eventually the deficit is paid down, there is a further key macroeconomic question to be answered. How can steadily rising demand be maintained without repeating the cyclical asset bubbles that provoked the financial crash in the first place? The origins of this problem derive from the evolution of capitalism after 1945. Initially the major barriers to capital accumulation were scarcity of labour both in Europe and in the US, together with the well-organised state of labour with political clout. Several strategies were implemented to deal with this.

First, the US in 1965 revised its immigration laws to allow access to the global surplus population, when previously Europeans and Caucasians were privileged. In the late 1960s the French began subsidising the import of labour from the Maghreb, the Germans brought in Turkish *Gastarbeiter*, the Swedes drew on the Yugoslavs, and the British imported labour from the empire. Second, there was a rapid surge in technological change which cut labour costs. Third, in the 1970s and 1980s right-wing leaders, notably Reagan, Thatcher and Pinochet, set about crushing organised labour. Fourthly, capital moved to find surplus labour by off-shoring, helped substantially at that time by the development of new transport strategies, particularly containerisation, which allowed cheap production of components in developing countries which could then be shipped at low cost to industrialised centres in the West for final assembly. Finally, in the 1980s and 1990s the sudden collapse of the Soviet Union and the transformation of much of China added a further two billion workers to the global workforce in twenty years.

However, this disempowerment of labour over the last thirty years has produced another central problem: if wages are repressed, this limits markets. It had two main consequences. One was that corporations sought to cover the gap between what labour was earning and what needed to be spent to maintain capital growth by allowing household indebtedness to rise dramatically through the credit card industry. Whereas in the 1980s average household debt in the US amounted to some $40,000, by 2008 this had risen to about $130,000 including mortgages. The mortgages were initially restricted to the 'respectable' working class, but by 2000 this market was becoming satiated and the drive to keep the process going increasingly led to sub-prime mortgages, with debt-financing of households with little or no income. The second consequence was that because of wage repression, the rich became far richer both relatively and absolutely. Because their immediate needs were satisfied, they invested in the stock market and bid up asset values including property and leisure facilities. Rather than generating new activity, they promoted stock market and property bubbles.

Given these dual pressures – labour purchasing power held down for competitive reasons and to enhance the rewards to capital, plus those enriched by the capitalist process increasingly directing their wealth into ostentatious consumption rather than productive investment – the problem of absorbing the capitalist surplus by generating an adequate level of overall demand has progressively intensified over time. In 1750 the global value of the total output of goods and services was around $135 billion, at constant values.[43] By 1950 it had risen to $4 trillion. By 2000 the rise had accelerated to $40 trillion, and it is now around $50 trillion, with some (e.g. Gordon Brown) predicting it will double to

---

43   Harvey, D., 'Their Crisis, Our Challenge', *Red Pepper*, March 2009.

$100 trillion by 2030. Throughout the history of capitalism the rate of growth has been close to 2.5 per cent a year compound. On that basis there would be a need by 2030 to find profitable outlets for $3 trillion. Given that under neo-liberal capitalism since the late 1970s less and less has been invested in real production and more and more has been put into speculation on asset value, that's a very tall order indeed. Even if the recent turn to financialisation (e.g. the development of complex derivatives in the City of London and Wall Street) to deal with the surplus absorption problem continued to be pursued, it couldn't work without periodic devalorisation (Schumpeter's 'creative destruction') of capital. Indeed, that necessary destruction of capital, with losses of several trillion dollars of asset value, is precisely the current post-2008 scenario.

Initially the enormous post-Second World War reconstruction fully absorbed the investment-seeking surplus in producing the quarter-century so-called Golden Age of capitalism (1948–73). But the faltering of net private non-residential fixed investment in the early 1970s signalled that the economy could no longer absorb all the investment-seeking surplus, and marked the onset of potentially deepening stagnation. Since then the problem has steadily worsened: nine out of the ten years with the lowest net private non-residential fixed investment as a percentage of the US GDP during the last half-century were in the 1990s and 2000s.

Three factors, however, have come into play which could reverse this process of stagnation. One has been the introduction of new technologies – notably the proliferation of computerisation, the internet, IT and digitalisation – but they have not produced comparable stimulus to earlier transformative technologies such as the car. The second has been soaring military spending. US war-related spending for the first time ever exceeded $1 trillion a year in 2008, double the level of the mid-1990s and larger than all other nations' military budgets combined. The supplementary US budget to fund the Iraq and Afghanistan wars, not part of the official defence budget, was still itself larger than the combined military budgets of Russia and China. Yet even this gargantuan level of US military spending has still not been sufficient to ward off stagnation.

Hence, capitalist economies have become increasingly dependent on the third factor, financialisation,[44] as a central vehicle of growth. Whereas previously finance did generate speculative excesses in the late stages of business cycle expansions, such episodes tended to be brief and leave no long-term effects on the structure and functioning of the economy. However, in the 1980s, not in a situation of overheating but rather of investment stagnation, a more independent financial sector increasingly attracted the funds of corporations and major investors. They were drawn especially by the egregiously high returns from the trade in the new exotic financial derivatives, notably structured investment vehicles. In particular these included collateralised debt obligation and credit default swaps, the global market in which had by the mid-2000s reached over $60 trillion, virtually equal to the value of world GDP.

By the 1990s and 2000s the artificial creation of immense asset bubbles had become the prime mechanism for driving demand in the Western economies. In the UK, even before Northern Rock collapsed in August 2007, leading to the wider banking crisis, the household debt bubble had reached £1.35 trillion, not far short

---

44   Foster, J. B., 'The Financialization of Capital and the Crisis', *Monthly Review*, April 2008.

of the level of the country's entire GDP. This process was taken even further by the rapid and enormous rise in private equity, hedge funds and widespread banking speculation and artificial tax avoidance where the objective was no longer investment in real production, but rather searching the world for the fastest short-term rewards for footloose 'hot money'. Such massive surges in capital speculation included the huge (and successful) gamble against the ERM in 1992, the sudden invasion of east Asian 'emerging markets' and equally abrupt exit in 1997–8, the dotcom bubble and bust in 1999–2000, and the property/credit financialisation bubble of 2004–8.

Given that there is now a financial surplus in the private sector of £3 trillion for the developed world in the balance sheets of private companies,[45] yet at the same time massive underinvestment leading to recession and rising unemployment, it is clear that the central problem lies in the gross deficiency of effective demand brought about by the steadily growing monopolisation of economic power in the hands of a hyper-rich elite whose interests no longer coincide with broad global economic development. That same growing disparity of control over capitalism's huge investable surplus has to be redressed by releasing the enormous scale of suppressed demand that the system has now produced, both among the long-term dispossessed in the developing countries and also in the growing impoverished segments of the populations in the developed world. But what this analysis shows above all is that capitalism in its extreme financialised form is utterly unsustainable and must be replaced by an alternative model which dramatically shifts remuneration, the basis of

---

45   Brown, G., *Beyond the Crash: Overcoming the First Crisis of Globalisation*, Simon & Schuster 2010.

future demand, towards the great mass of the population whose purchasing power has perennially been artificially suppressed. That imperative for the survival of the capitalist system will also be the most powerful driver towards its transformation. We will return to this in Chapter XII.

CHAPTER IX

THE MAJOR REVIVAL OF MANUFACTURING HOLDS THE KEY

(I) WHY REACTIVATING NEO-LIBERALISM AFTER THE GREAT CRASH WON'T WORK

Despite the profound failures of neo-liberal capitalism spelt out in Chapter VI, the response from the same political and financial elite who generated the global 2008–9 financial–economic breakdown has been to try to restart the same engine all over again. There are both proximate as well as deeper structural reasons, however, why this default position will not work, and why fresh policies based on fundamentally different foundations are now therefore necessary, if not inevitable.

The roots of the crisis stretch back to 1998 when the hedge fund Long-Term Capital Management imploded. The rescue by the US Fed ensured that the reckless dotcom boom of the late 1990s continued for another two years, and when the internet bubble finally collapsed in the face of wild overvaluations and falling profitability, the Fed charged to the rescue once again. Interest rates were sliced to 1 per cent and left there for a year, which generated the biggest US housing boom ever. When the Fed finally tightened monetary policy, it was too late. The biggest bubble in history led to the biggest bust in history, and then a policy extravaganza to match. Yet despite the deployment of near-zero interest rates kept in place for years, electronic money creation on a colossal and unprecedented scale (£375 billion in the UK, and rising), and manipulation of the money markets (the LIBOR interest rate-fixing scandal finally wrecking the City's hold over policy), still recovery in both the US and the UK has proved elusive.

The lessons of this failure go much deeper. Over the last few decades an ever bigger stimulus has been required to generate a growth spurt. Even when growth is finally stimulated, the upswings have been weaker than in the quarter-century after the Second World War, and the trade deficits triggered have been larger. Moreover, prior to 1980 incomes grew alongside economic growth, productivity improvements benefited everyone, manufacturing employment rose and the trade deficit was negligible.[46] But after 1980 the gains from productivity were usurped by those on the topmost incomes, manufacturing jobs were lost even during upswings, and the 2001–7 boom was the weakest in post-war history. After 1980 the growth paradigm entailed squeezing worker incomes, contracting household savings rates, pushing up debt levels, generating persistent asset price inflation above consumer price inflation, and relying on ever lower nominal (i.e. unadjusted for inflation) interest rates. It is true that much of this was for too long concealed by asset price bubbles, low-cost imports, financial innovation and cheap money. But there are limits to how high debt levels can reach or how low interest rates can fall in order to maintain an unsustainable model. After the Great Crash this is not a viable paradigm to return to.

---

46   Palley, T., *From Financial Crisis to Stagnation: The Destruction of Shared Prosperity and the Role of Economics*, Cambridge University Press, 2012.

There is an even bigger reason to abandon this model. Britain cannot continue indefinitely with balance of payments deficits rising inexorably year after year. The last time Britain had a current account surplus was in 1983, twenty-nine years ago. In the last fifty-five years Britain has only had a surplus on its traded goods in six years. Initially in the 1970s the surplus in services (insurance, shipping etc. as well as banking) covered the deficit in goods, but from 1987 the deficit in goods rose much more sharply and a large net deficit between goods and services grew ever wider. By 2010 the deficit in traded goods had reached the staggering level of £99 billion and the surplus on services at £49 billion could cover only half of this. A yawning deficit of this magnitude cannot continue for long without the creditors (like any bank manager) calling time. It is equally clear that services, valuable as they are to the British economy, cannot on their own arrest this continuing, even accelerating, decline. There is only one way in which it can be reversed, and that is by addressing the real cause of the collapse via a major and sustained revitalisation of UK manufacturing capacity. The remainder of this chapter sets out how this should be done.

(2) THE IMPORTANCE OF MANUFACTURING TO BRITAIN

Contrary to general perception Britain is still a major manufacturing economy – in fact, the sixth largest in the world. Though its share in UK economic activity has fallen steeply from 35 per cent in 1970 to 11 per cent in 2010 and its number of jobs has declined from over 6.6 million in 1979 to under 2.5 million in 2010, its output has risen steadily and is now actually 9.5 per cent higher than in 1979, reflecting the rapid growth in labour productivity in UK manufacturing, which has outstripped productivity growth in the rest of the economy by 55 per cent since 1993.[47] It now accounts for less than one in ten jobs in the UK today, and some have attributed this to a shift towards high-tech manufacturing as the UK's low-tech manufacturing base is eroded by overseas competition, particularly from China. However, ONS Labour Force Survey figures show that the high- and medium-high-tech manufacturing sector shed jobs twice as fast during the 2007–10 recession as the low-tech manufacturing base. But despite the sharp contraction during the recession, manufacturing bounced back strongly in 2010, again outperforming the economy as a whole.

Despite the lingering image of dark satanic mills and dirty noisy workplaces, UK manufacturing is today often highly automated, with skilled employees working flexibly in clean, dust-free environments. Within the wider global network, Britain's competitive edge is increasingly found in innovation by companies that are part of global supply chains where the final mass production and assembly is transferred to emerging markets, for tax reasons as well as lower wage costs. And as the borderline between manufacturing and services blurs, providing services to customers is increasingly part of the business for manufacturers. This is sometimes referred to as the rise in manu-services, embracing specialised staff from research scientists and designers to marketing executives and support engineers, and involving a very different economic model. Instead of buying and owning a good, the customer often pays a regular fee to rent it or derive a service from the good. Longer service contracts replace a series of one-off transactions, and risk may well be redistributed back to the producer of the product. Manufacturers devote time and

47   ONS Labour Market Statistics, Gross Value Added figures, BIS, and ONS Productivity Time Series.

effort to developing relationships with customers, often leading to greater customer involvement in designing and producing goods (bespoke manufacturing). As a result manufacturing firms now generate 15–20 per cent of their revenues from services, thus making manu-services responsible for some 2 per cent of UK GDP, about the same as all UK lawyers and accountants.

Manufacturing is crucial to Britain in many important ways. First, it makes a key contribution to combating the UK's serious trade deficit. In 2009, 58 per cent of UK exports were goods, mainly manufactures, and because manufacturing is more export oriented than other sectors of the economy, only a strong manufacturing sector can redress Britain's chronic trade imbalance, which has been in deficit every year since 1997. The size of this task is shown by the fact that despite a 23 per cent exchange rate devaluation between early 2007 and the end of 2010, the UK deficit worsened considerably, averaging over £4 billion a month in the second half of 2010. Indeed, Coutts and Rowthorn have argued that the UK trade deficit is now a permanent trend caused by the imbalanced structure of the economy, leading to a strategic trade deficit equal to 4.7 per cent of GDP unless there are fundamental changes to the foundations of the economy.[48]

Second, the manufacturing industry is a major investor in intangible assets such as R&D, design and brand equity which help to create the ideas and technologies to support the knowledge economy. NESTA research reveals that UK manufacturing companies invest 20 per cent of their value-added in intangibles, amounting to more than £35 billion a year.[49] At the same

---

48   Coutts, K. and Rowthorn, R., *Prospects for the UK Balance of Payments*, Civitas, March 2010.
49   Haskel, J. et al., *Driving Economic Growth: Innovation, Knowledge Spending and Productivity Growth in the UK*, NESTA, January 2011.

time the sector spends £12 billion a year on tangible assets, so that the ratio of intangible to tangible investment is 3:1, while in the wider economy it is only 1.6:1, and this ratio has been steadily increasing for manufacturing firms over the last decade. This is particularly the case in respect of R&D and design: of the top twenty-five companies by R&D spending, sixteen are from the manufacturing sector. This significant investment in intangibles means that manufacturing is responsible for some 42 per cent of innovation in the UK's market sector, a very important contribution to the UK knowledge economy.

Third, manufacturing stimulates demand in other UK economic sectors, in particular helping to support businesses in the service sector. ONS figures show that the manufacturing industry spends about £75 billion a year on goods and services from other economic sectors, around 5 per cent of total UK GDP.[50] Of this spending, half is on knowledge-intensive business services, thus benefiting businesses that primarily sell intangible assets.

Fourth, while manufacturing is now largely a global business, the UK remains successful in capturing large parts of the value created through global supply chains. For example, British silicon chips appear in iPods, games consoles and mobile telephones that are marked as products of China or other emerging markets. In other sectors which depend on advanced scientific and engineering skills, like pharmaceuticals, life sciences and aerospace, Britain still retains a world leadership. The scale of inward foreign direct investment is higher for Britain than for any other country in Europe, *inter alia* reviving the UK's role as a major car manufacturer. Altogether UK manufacturing provides

---

50   ONS, Supply and Use Tables, 2008.

around half of UK export earnings, while financial services account for only an eighth. Almost half of all jobs in UK manufacturing are in management or service occupations, yet even in low- and medium-tech manufacturing Britain retains a strong base through efficient production, rapid and reliable delivery, and adding services to products.

(3) TACKLING THE WEAKNESSES IN BRITISH MANUFACTURING

So UK manufacturing industry, belying its stereotype, is in no way old fashioned, declining or a residue from the past; it's mostly high-tech, dynamic, innovative and the essential core to the British economy. Nevertheless there remain serious weaknesses which undermine its competitive potential, and these need to be systematically addressed as a priority for Britain.

(i) The need for a larger flow of qualified, skilled workers

The shortage of skills needed for the manufacturing industry has been endemic in the UK for perhaps 150 years. The UK has never promoted an effective technical education system with parity of esteem with universities and 'higher' education because the prejudice of academic distinction has always remained strong among Britain's ruling elite. A range of quangos, advisory bodies and watchdogs has presided over a limited development of apprenticeships and technical qualifications, but that has never produced the flow of skilled workers that manufacturing needs in a modern labour market where the skills and motivation of the workforce are a force for competitive advantage. Importing immigrant labour from eastern Europe or wider overseas sources is no adequate substitute when the skills are rarely high-tech and supply does not match demand in any stable or sustainable manner. The current system of technical training has been designed around improving skills by driving up the range of qualifications, which can therefore be rigidly structured and which does not necessarily meet employers' needs.

Closer consultation is needed with employers in each main industrial sector to ensure that technical training is demand led, but it should also be a requirement on employers in all medium and large companies to provide high-quality apprenticeships and skill training related to their own needs, funded by at least a minimum percentage of turnover. Britain's shortfall relative to Germany's is very striking: Britain currently has some 491,300 apprentices compared to Germany's 1.6 million, and apprenticeship starts, which have been steadily rising in the UK over the last fifteen years, are still, at 279,700 in 2010, only half the German rate. Furthermore, apprenticeship training in Germany is more intensive, embraces as many as two-thirds of all young people after compulsory education, and over a three-year period involves a dual system of vocational education in both a company and a vocational college. In addition the Federal Training Institute (FTI) is responsible for ensuring that the training in the vocational school and in the host company are complementary, often involving extensive negotiations between the FTI and employer representatives on the content, examination requirements and overall objectives of each apprenticeship. It is a highly successful model which could well be replicated in the UK given the latter's serious dearth of apprenticeships over the last three decades.

At an earlier stage the supply of skilled workers should be greatly improved by ensuring that secondary schools generate a greater flow of able and motivated young people, when at present too many leave school with few or no qualifications, no aspirations and no awareness of the world of work around them. Of particular concern to manufacturers is the slippage in standards in science and technology education in schools and universities. The academic rigour of secondary school examinations has been greatly diluted and the numbers studying science subjects have been artificially inflated by including such courses as sports sciences and arts-based psychology. All children should be required to study the traditional separate science GCSEs whatever school they attend, and the academic underpinning for all STEM subjects should be restored and then over time steadily raised. In addition, the Diploma programme, which was meant to offer a viable and effective post-fourteen vocational route in schools but has not gained the intended traction with this age group, should be greatly simplified, cut from four levels to two, and made less specialised but with a stronger work experience component.

On R&D spending, a seminal US study has questioned whether paying subsidies to companies is the best means to promote innovation, rather than further investment in the science base.[51] Phasing out the £600 million R&D tax credit currently paid to large companies would fund an increased supply of scientists, strengthen links between researchers and businesses as in the German Fraunhofer networks, and allow Whitehall better to stimulate innovation through government procurement programmes.

Government should also put resources and effort into creating a political culture that supports innovation and industry, to counter the false and damaging image of manufacturing as old-fashioned, poorly paid and unpleasant work, which discourages

---

51   Romer, P., 'Should the Government Subsidize Supply and Demand in the Market for Scientists and Engineers?', NBER Working Paper 7723, 2000.

able young adults from considering jobs that are actually increasingly highly skilled and well paid. This means raising the profile of manufacturing in the national consciousness and reshaping the negative image of industry in the media. It should also increase the currently inadequate funding for the Manufacturing Insight programme, which aims to give secondary school children, their teachers and their parents a fairer and more realistic view of what manufacturing is really like. The broadcasting media, which at present focuses mainly on the health service, the law and the police, should also be encouraged to consider the importance of manufacturing and its potentially exciting challenges.

(ii) Access to finance

Raising finance for entrepreneurial activity continues to be problematic for many reasons. Bank lending to manufacturers, especially small businesses, is often hard to come by, especially in a recession, when it is most needed, most notably in 2010–12. The City of London remains heavily focused on mortgage lending, derivatives and offshore speculation, and during the 2007–11 recession the M4 money supply for business lending collapsed to near-zero annual growth. Though continuation of lending at 2007 levels was a condition of the government bail-out, banks opted instead to consolidate their balance sheets. Clearly there is a gap in the market for specialised banks focused on small businesses, manu-services and green investments, and given the anti-competitive hold on the finance market by the Big Four, public sector banks should be established to meet these needs.

A more durable problem with bank lending to UK manufacturing is its short-termism. Many banks lend on a one-off basis for a specific project on a limited timescale, and therefore expect high annual returns on investments to meet their loan repayments, which often appear too risky in uncertain market conditions. Rigour in assessing funding applications is certainly vital, but in most cases should take place in the context of an ongoing long-term relationship between the bank and its main customers. This relational banking is one central factor underpinning German manufacturing success, linked with the clustering concept of the *Mittelstand* offering a strong local or regional network uniting major interacting manufacturing companies with their suppliers, ancillaries and customers as well as their banks. This is a business model in Baden-Württemberg, Emilia-Romagna and other European regions which the UK should develop in manufacturing arcs round Birmingham, Manchester, Liverpool and Newcastle as well as the south-east.

(iii) Safeguarding strategic manufacturing sectors

A more contentious but very necessary area for government partnership with manufacturing concerns the assertion of the national interest in preserving industries and companies integral to Britain's economic survival. The disastrous consequences of leaving Britain's key industries and strategic companies uninhibitedly exposed to acquisition in the international market (a laissez-faire policy that no other major country follows) were spelt out in Chapter V (2).

Currently Britain's openness to FDI has attracted major overseas manufacturers like (US) Ford, General Motors, General Electric, (German) Siemens, (Indian) Tata, and the big three Japanese car-makers. This is justified on the grounds that they are claimed to be larger and more efficient and to invest more per employee than UK counterparts. On the other hand, the attraction is largely as a base for export to the EU market and because costs are lower through low pay and deregulated working conditions. In addition R&D is generally centred abroad and profits are largely repatriated to the home country. This is not an adequate platform on which to build a dynamic, competitive and sustainable manufacturing base as the core of UK economic growth. UK policy needs to strike a balance between market freedom wherever possible within which entrepreneurs and innovators can flourish and safeguarding UK control over strategic sectors which are critical to the consolidation of an essential UK economic base. Both protectionism and national defence-lessness are to be resisted, and a course that steers between them is the right one.

Equally the role of hedge funds and private equity in distorting the national interest in favour of private greed has to be tackled. The business model that exploits property values against the intrinsic value of the company's products or services, as deployed recently for example against Debenhams, Boots, the AA, Focus DIY and Southern Cross, should be curtailed. Buying a company (usually with borrowed money) to obtain maximum value extraction by selling off its freehold properties (often at a profit in excess of £1 billion shared between a small clique of investors), then overloading the company with debt by leasing back the properties at high rents which are paid for by 'sweating the assets' (usually job cuts, pay restraint, longer hours and harder working conditions), is not a tactic designed to improve Britain's economic performance, and should be squeezed out by regulation. What Britain needs in each sector is the development of committed long-term relationships between finance and industry designed to increase market share, not short-term in-and-out purchases that cream off easy profits and then exit with a rapid sale.

Equally, private equity buying up shares en masse of a target company at a late stage in a contested takeover bid, which, for example, tipped the balance in the 2010 Kraft takeover of Cadbury, is not in the public interest. It is rather the maximisation of short-term private gain whatever the loss to the national interest, and as such should be blocked. Again, 'shorting', by buying up shares targeted for a fall in a company's share price and then offloading the shares in bulk as the price falls to cream off the maximum private gain (or even more, 'naked shorting', where the shares are not even bought, but temporarily leased for a rent) is about stripping out short-term private gain without regard to building up Britain's economic strength, and should be prevented. These are the tactics of the stock market casino, the elevation of financial engineering over real engineering. More generally, the abuses created by these agglomerations of private economic power in the hands of hedge funds and private equity, and the remedies needed, are set out in the two following chapters on finance.

(iv) The restoration of crucial supply chains

Britain's broken supply chains, as detailed at length in Chapter V(2), undermine high UK content and limit backward linkages to domestic suppliers because much of the higher-level spend on components and other intermediate products leaks abroad. In the UK the propensity to import is much higher, largely because of reliance on foreign-owned assembly within global systems – for example for British machinery and vehicles 50 per cent of intermediate purchases are imported, compared with 30 per cent in Germany. It is true that some new corporate exemplars (e.g. ARM in chips for smart products or Dyson in vacuum cleaners) have adapted to broken supply chains by outsourcing everything except design and chain organisation, though this is less a solution than a temporary respite from continuing structural decline via enforced adaptation.

What is needed is a sustained rise in manufacturing output which can break this long-run trend of flat output since the 1970s, which brought with it falling employment as productivity increased, and to achieve this against the background of the internal problem of broken national supply chains and the external pressure of tough competition from Germany, China and Japan. The urgency of this problem is exacerbated by the degree and speed with which Britain's output gap, already very serious, is getting worse. It has been estimated that even if all UK domestically produced manufactures (including exports) were consumed in the UK, it would still only meet four-fifths of total domestic demand.

In addition, Coutts and Rowthorn[52] in their detailed study of the UK's balance of trade prospects project an unsustainable increase in the UK deficit which will limit macroeconomic policy options and require permanent deflation to damp down import demand. All these entrenched problems point to the need for policies to encourage capacity-building and investment right across the spectrum in manufacturing. There are several policies that could assist. Manufacturers' corporation tax could be reduced for every year that they increase output (excluding output generated by overseas subsidiaries or sub-contractors) by more than 3 per cent, the historic manufacturing productivity

---

52   Coutts, K. and Rowthorn, R., *Prospects for the UK Balance of Payments*, Civitas, March 2010.

growth rate. Investment could be promoted by enhanced depreciation allowances. And new manufacturing jobs could be incentivised by a national insurance holiday for each additional new worker, tapered over, say, three years.

(v) Driving innovation

It has been estimated that innovation was responsible for two-thirds of UK labour productivity growth between 2000 and 2007, and increasingly from non-traditional sources. Of the £133 billion invested by the private sector in innovation in 2007,[53] traditional scientific R&D accounted for only 11 per cent. Most included investment needed to commercialise ideas – product design, training in new skills, organisational innovation, developing branding and copyright. Significantly, this applies to all sectors, not just high-tech ones. The fastest-growing 6 per cent of businesses generated half of the jobs created by existing businesses in the UK between 2002 and 2008, and these companies were found in all economic sectors and in all regions. Nor is the British manufacturing share of total GVA (gross value added as a measure of productivity and innovation), at 13 per cent in the UK compared with 22 per cent in Germany, as poor as its traducers make out. Once the size of the sector is controlled for (nearly twice as large in Germany as in the UK), the UK manufacturing sector produces more value-added than Germany's both in output and employee share terms. UK manufacturing, so far from being a busted flush as it is sometimes condescendingly disparaged, in fact more than holds its own against Europe's manufacturing powerhouse, though on a smaller scale.

---

53   'The Innovation Index', NESTA, November 2009.

The problem, however, lies in the long tail of low-tech UK industries (28 per cent in low- and medium-low-tech, compared with 24 per cent in the US and 17 per cent in Japan), which are critically vulnerable to Asian competition and will only survive and flourish if they move up the value chain to the higher end of the medium-tech segment, where the UK share is currently below the EU12 average and far below Germany's, most notably in the car industry. The reasons for this include the ready availability of low-cost workers, unenterprising management unready to shift to high-value-added product strategies, funding constraints and skill deficiencies.[54] Each of these needs urgent attention. In particular, a significant increase in the national minimum wage is needed (quite apart from the social equity grounds) to incentivise firms to upgrade their workforce skills, boost productivity, and reduce employers' fall-back onto state wage subsidies like the working tax credit. Research by the OECD indicates that higher minimum wages generate higher productivity in low-wage industries as firms replace unskilled with skilled workers, with no overall impact on unemployment.[55]

(vi) Institutions to develop long-termism

The reason why short-termism is so deeply entrenched in the British business culture is that the institutions of neo-liberal capitalism require it. Corporate governance is characterised by the shareholder model of equity finance, well-developed venture capital markets, and a relaxed attitude to hostile takeovers by the competition authorities. Managers therefore have to pay careful

---

54   Coulter, S., *Manufacturing Prosperity: Diversifying UK Economic Growth*, Social Market Foundation, March 2011, p. 23.
55   Bassanini, A. and Venn, D., 'The Impact of Labour Market Policies on Productivity in OECD Countries', *International Productivity Monitor*, Fall 2008, p. 8.

attention to maintaining their company's share price and current profitability, enforcing a strictly short-term approach. This same perspective pervades all other aspects of the system. Labour markets are unstable, with minimum regulation, leaving unions weak (less than 15 per cent coverage of the private sector workforce in Britain) and creating unfettered space for management autonomy, encouraging a short-term instrumentalist attitude to worker value and individual security. Vocational training is geared towards flexible transferable skills, with a minimum safety net welfare state aimed to pressurise workers into taking any jobs available. Markets are highly competitive, governed by formal contracting and technology transfer achieved by poaching staff.

It is difficult, if not impossible, to remove the short-termism inherent in the structure of neo-liberalism without quite fundamentally changing the system itself. The long-term perspective is built rather into the Rhenish (as opposed to Anglo-Saxon) genre of capitalism, and that is characterised by a more egalitarian and consensual approach to economics and social justice. This is the contrasting stakeholder model of governance, with a relational banking partnership (most notably the German *Hausbanks*) and disapproval of hostile takeovers. Inter-firm co-ordination takes precedence over generating innovation and setting standards, and the incremental nature of innovation offers continuous improvements in existing technologies. Extensive collaboration between management and workers enhances loyalty to the firm and minimises disruption, while allowing workers (and their powerful centralised trade unions) a major say in key decisions on the future of the firm, and protecting workers against arbitrary hire and fire. Employees are more highly valued and a stronger training system, firm centred and co-ordinated by industry associations, generates good-quality technical and industry-specific skills.

These two contrasting systems offer different strengths and weaknesses. Neo-liberal market economies will tend to focus on highly innovative, high-tech fast-moving sectors (e.g. biotechnology, software development, IT and financial services), but also with a long tail in price-sensitive, low-value-added goods, while at the same time lacking access to the 'patient' capital necessary for long-term restructuring and lacking inter-firm collaboration necessary for continuous product development. Co-ordinated market economies, on the other hand, and in particular the Modell Deutschland, are prone to a weak service sector, an 'insider–outsider' labour market which discriminates against those left out of the employment mainstream, low female participation and a failure to generate high-tech industrial clusters. The central point, however, for promoting the long-term perspective as a key ingredient in a successful manufacturing strategy is that it requires a positive institutional environment to embed it at every level, and only the co-ordinated market structures of stakeholder capitalism are likely to entrench long-termism with the intensity and ubiquity that is needed.

CHAPTER X

REBALANCING THE ECONOMY

(I) REPAIRING A BADLY DISLOCATED ECONOMIC STRUCTURE

If the emphasis within the UK economy needs to move decisively towards a major manufacturing recovery, how is this 'rebalancing', much talked about but little acted upon, to be achieved? Rebalancing is a novel trope which has many topical applications – trade-based (the growing gap between imports and exports), fiscal (the unsustainable size of the national budget deficit and private household debt), sectoral (the relative roles of the public and private sectors), regional (the south-east versus the rest of the country), and economic components (manufacturing versus finance). The last, which is of chief concern here, has been very marked over the last forty years. The numbers employed in British manufacturing declined every year from 7.9 million in 1971 to 2.7 million in 2008, while the numbers employed in finance over the same period rose slowly from 0.6 million to 1.1 million. But by 2008 finance, which still accounted for less than 4 per cent of the total British workforce, had increased its share of output to 9.1 per cent and its share of profits to 12.8 per cent. However, at that point the financial bubble burst and it became clear that gambling on derivatives and other massive overseas speculation did not constitute a firm foundation for UK economic growth. The search for an alternative to manufacturing as the powerhouse of the economy was shattered.

The UK finance sector is oversized for its primary role of servicing UK businesses and households: it is twice the size relative to GDP of comparable finance sectors in the EU. Its size is usually eulogised because of the benefit accruing to the Exchequer from the annual £25 billion tax revenue. But that is to ignore three substantial drawbacks – the cost to taxpayers of a major financial crash running into hundreds of billions of pounds;[56] the crowding out of small business, industry and manufacturing funding needs by the big banks' fixation on quick-profit international speculation; and an overvalued exchange rate which favours City investments abroad over manufacturing needs at home. As the City has grown in size and importance, more of UK manufacturing has been exported overseas. The national priority must clearly now instead be to expand both national and local businesses as the core foundation of Britain's manufacturing and industry on which the long-term economic sustainability of the UK depends. That expansion will only come about if the biggest banks, whose predilection is so strongly towards high-risk speculation and short-term profiteering abroad with footloose capital, are broken up and operate differently, more like banks in Germany and Japan in supporting business. Britain needs smaller banks and, specifically, specialist business banks focusing on infrastructure, housing, a green de-carbonised economy, creative industries, science and R&D etc.

But can a renaissance of manufacturing be achieved, in

---

56   Even if the £25 billion-a-year payments to the Exchequer continued, which they certainly will not, it would take sixty years of payments at that rate to pay back the increase in national debt to an expected £1.4 trillion by 2015 which the financial crash caused.

particular by the faster growth of other sectors rather than simply by the downsizing of finance? On the basis of trends over the last four decades it seems unlikely. The British economy boomed 2002–7, but there was no cyclical upturn in UK manufacturing output as there had been in the general economic recoveries of the 1980s and 1990s. A 25–30 per cent depreciation of the pound against the euro then drove British export sales briefly, but the long-term steady shift in the relative value of the pound to the euro from €2.23 in 1970 to €1.10 in 2011 suggests UK export performance is now overdependent on continuous depreciation. It is highly disturbing that when sterling, after reaching its peak in mid-2007, then became relatively weak, the current account 'recovery' had stalled by the end of 2009 and then started to widen again. This persistence in high current account deficits despite a weaker pound indicates that the fundamental imbalance in the British economy has now reached a point where even a substantial devaluation cannot remedy it.

The current account balance has been in deficit for all but eighteen of the last sixty-five years, but this conceals the seriousness of the deterioration in the balance of trade in goods, which has accelerated very sharply in the neo-liberal era of the last three decades from a surplus of £1.3 billion in 1980 to a deficit of £98.8 billion in 2010, equal to 6.8 per cent of Britain's GDP. This was significantly offset by a rising surplus in the trade in services over the same period, more than covering the deficit in goods until 1987 but by 2010 covering only half the gap, which had soared to £49 billion or 3.4 per cent of GDP. This growing overall deficit in the current account has then been offset by surpluses in the capital account (mainly general government capital payments to, or receipts from, institutions such as the EU) since 1982, and more so by the financial account (i.e. transactions in direct and portfolio investment and in financial derivatives and reserve assets) since 1987. What this indicates is that Britain's balance of payments deficits are only sustainable so long as overseas companies and governments are willing to purchase UK assets, including holding UK sterling reserves, with the sterling they earn from selling goods and services for UK consumption. Long-term (or even medium-term), this is clearly an untenable position.

Analysis of trends in UK manufacturing over the last three decades reveals further evidence of the growing precariousness of the country's economic foundations. While expenditure on innovation (R&D) by all UK companies doubled at current prices from £8 billion in 1990 to £15.6 billion in 2009 (though representing a relative decline from 1.4 per cent to 1.1 per cent of GDP), expenditure on mergers and acquisitions (M&A) over the same period more than trebled from £21 billion to an estimated £69 billion in 2011.[57] Even more remarkably, M&A expenditure rocketed six-fold from £46 billion in 1997 to no less than £288 billion in 2000 before falling back and then rising again sharply to £85 billion in 2007. Another facet of this M&A boom has been that in periods when it is rising fast, it is disproportionately directed overseas. It is forecast that while £7 billion will have been devoted to UK acquisitions in 2011, £62 billion will have been directed abroad.

Furthermore, while these trends relate to the UK economy as a whole, for UK manufacturing they are much more disturbing. The proportion of profit (gross operating surplus) accounted for by manufacturing companies fell from 33 per cent of all UK

---

57   National Statistics (ONS) database series DLBX, DLHT, DLEP, DLEX.

private non-financial corporations over the last two decades to just 13 per cent in 2010, and the proportion of gross capital employed accounted for by manufacturing fell over the same period similarly from more than a third compared to all UK non-financial companies to less than a fifth. In addition, expenditure on R&D in manufacturing has consistently been lower than in UK businesses generally, and fell over this same period from 1.1 per cent to the very low level of 0.8 per cent of GDP by 2009.

(2) SHIFTING BRITAIN'S FINANCE FLOWS TO PROMOTE SUSTAINABLE RECOVERY

At present the allocation of capital and income in the British economy is severely counter-productive. Too much ends up in speculative finance and not nearly enough in productive manufacturing investment. Too much is creamed off by a 2–5 per cent rich elite who fritter their money on luxuries, and far too little goes to the lower-paid third to a half of the population whose greater spend, if available, would drive domestic economic growth. Far too much demand is artificially created by mountains of household debt, rather than redressing the vast and still growing inequalities of income that give rise to it. Far too great distortions are made in the tax system in favour of capital, tax breaks and leniency towards tax avoidance which favour rich individuals and big corporations, and too little is afforded to small- and medium-scale enterprise, innovation and technology. Too great rewards are allocated to short-term profiteering and not nearly enough to long-term investment and commitment to market share. This requires a huge programme of reform, but every one of these misallocations needs to be reversed.

(i) From finance to manufacturing

First, private equity and hedge funds, huge aggregations of private economic power ruthlessly geared to maximise short-term economic gains irrespective of the wider public interest, remain grossly under-taxed after the successive loopholes granted by Brown in the early 2000s. Their accounts should be made fully transparent on a nationwide basis, the loophole allowing income to be transposed into capital gains at a lower rate of tax should be closed, short-term capital gains (i.e. less than five years) should be chargeable to tax at a higher rate of 60 per cent, and a proportion of their funds should be required to be placed for a minimum five-year period into domestic industrial investments of priority national importance. Similarly, it is not sufficient merely to split investment banks from their retail counterparts, even if the Vickers 'Chinese walls' achieved this (which they won't). The UK cannot afford the dissipation of their huge funding streams on speculative short-term or over-risky excesses, as in recent derivatives trading. Such activities, where not prohibited, should be subject to a high premium tax of 60 per cent on any gains. Again, they would be expected to prioritise internal UK investments, encouraged by a significantly lower rate of tax on long-term investments of approved national importance.

The substantial extra funding thus released could be transferred from finance to strengthen and reinvigorate key areas of manufacturing. Existing financial support for start-ups like the Enterprise Management Incentive, Enterprise Investment Scheme and the Early Growth Funds often turn out to be too small or too regionally focused to achieve the necessary impact. Venture capital for the next stage of development, requiring an input between £2 million and £10 million, can also be hard to obtain, and the Rowlands report recently recommended creating a new form of mezzanine finance aimed at companies needing capital at this level. Perhaps the most effective assistance, however, that government can give would be to ensure there were no further cuts in capital allowances, while also allowing capital expenditure to be written off in full over eight years.[58]

The additional funding could also be used to restructure the financing of industry. Clearly there is a gap in the market for specialised banks focused on small businesses, manu-services and green investments, and given the anti-competitive hold on the finance market by the Big Four, public sector banks should be established to meet these needs. In addition, to counter short-termism, future funding for industry should be conducted in the context of an ongoing long-term relationship between the bank and its main customers.

(ii) From a luxuried elite to the relatively impoverished core

A second serious misallocation of the country's financial resources arises from the huge distortion over the last thirty years in income distribution. The share of wages in GDP, driven by technological change, outsourcing and globalisation, fell from 65.1 per cent in 1975 to 53 per cent in 1995, and remained at 53.2 per cent in 2007, a post-war low. The share of profits in GDP, largely concentrated on top managers and rich investors and shareholders, correspondingly increased. Within the declining share of wages, pay at the top escalated dramatically towards the end of this period, with a typical FTSE 100 chief executive

---

58 Willman, J., *Innovation and Industry: A Manifesto for Manufacturing*, Policy Exchange, 2010, p. 36.

being paid thirty-nine times the national average in 2000, but nearly 200 times in 2010. At the same time, middle and low incomes stagnated or fell throughout the 2005–15 decade.

The macroeconomic consequences of this skewing of demand have been stark. The super-rich have generally been more adept at redistributing existing wealth than creating new wealth. Soaring corporate pay at the top has not brought about any significant improvement in UK productivity and innovation. Britain has not closed its long-standing productivity gap with its major competitors since output per worker remains almost 40 per cent below US levels and 20 per cent below France and Germany. Though there are many reasons for this, certainly one of them is the comparative lack of business innovation, with Britain continuing to be placed low in the international entrepreneurial league.[59] Among OECD countries only the UK had a lower share of GDP spent on R&D in 2000 than in 1981.

It is often argued that the huge increase in wealth at the top 'trickles down' to benefit the rest of society. The evidence, however, is that any gain peters out quickly as it descends the income scale and is largely confined to the affluent. The super-wealthy have certainly generated booming markets for designer clothes, exotic holidays, exclusive restaurants, bespoke jewellery, luxury yachts and lifestyle management gurus, as well as an army of legal and financial advisers and general fixers. Contemporary art prices quadrupled in the decade to 2007, order books for private jets and premium cars were full for years ahead, and property prices soared, driven by expanding City bonuses and

---

59   Hay, M. et al., Entrepreneurship Monitor, London Business School, 2006; and Robert Huggins Associates, World Knowledge Competitiveness Index, 2005.

the arrival of super-rich foreigners drawn by their non-domicile tax-free status and lower stamp duty from placing homes in offshore companies.

But the downsides have been far greater. The boom in property wealth strangled housing choices for ordinary people, particularly young first-time buyers, with low-cost housing, schools, pubs and petrol stations pulled down to make way for prestigious luxury flats and executive penthouses. The regional gap has widened sharply as the industrial north can no longer, as in Victorian times, counter the growing power of the London-based plutocracy. The polarisation of wealth, particularly in hyper-capitalist London but in other cities too, is driving the same degree of social disintegration from jobless despair to burgeoning crime to poorer health to growing homelessness, as was previously witnessed in the Edwardian era and the 'roaring twenties' just prior to the Great Crash. But above all the suppression of demand among the majority of the population through three decades of relatively falling incomes followed by a decade of an absolute fall in living standards has grossly diverted the economy towards satisfying the niche markets for extravagant fripperies at the expense of the mainstream productive investment on which the nation's economic future depends.

(iii) From unproductive to productive investment

In 2010 a mere 8 per cent of net lending by UK banks went to productive investment (i.e. manufacturing, construction, communications, distribution, retail and wholesale). No less than eleven-twelfths of their lending was devoted to real estate and business services, financial intermediation, public and other services, and mortgages, much of it involving foreign and speculative investment.[60] The motive behind this discrimination against business investment is that a large bank will usually prefer to loan against collateral – a house that can be repossessed – rather than against the risk and uncertainty of future cash flows. A market intervention is needed to alter these incentives, and one that has worked successfully in the past. In the 1960s informal guidance for bank credit by the central bank, known as 'moral suasion', limited the amount of credit banks could create and set quotas for specific sectors. This guidance on the direction of lending always accorded priority to export finance.

Some of the most successful countries after the Second World War also employed direct credit controls to launch their economies on a virtuous spiral of export expansion. Using 'window guidance' the central banks of Japan, Korea and Taiwan determined the desired nominal GDP growth, then calculated the necessary amount of credit creation to achieve this target, and then allocated this credit across different banks and industrial sectors.[61] Under this system unproductive credit creation was suppressed. In particular, credit for speculative transactions, such as the present extensive UK bank lending to hedge funds, was hard to obtain. Equally, large-scale consumer loans were restricted since this could draw in imports and bolster consumer price inflation. Most bank credit was allocated to productive use, whether in the form of investment in plant and equipment or to offer more services or to enhance productivity via new technologies and R&D. This intervention in credit allocation was widely recognised to underpin the east Asian economic miracle. Japanese-style window

60   Bank of England Statistical Interactive Database.
61   Ryan-Collins, J., Greenham, T., Werner, R. and Jackson, A., *Where Does Money Come From?: A Guide to the UK Monetary and Banking System*, New Economics Foundation, 2011.

guidance was also adopted by China in the Deng Xiaoping reforms of the 1980s, which laid the foundations of the very high and sustained economic growth that did not fall foul either of the Asian economic crisis in the late 1990s or of the global banking crisis of 2008. Credit guidance therefore has a proven record for delivering stable and sustainable economic growth.

By contrast, unregulated control of the money supply in the hands of the commercial banks has generated successive asset bubbles in the UK which have destabilised the economy and, when they have imploded, caused colossal costs to the taxpayer (£70 billion in direct bail-outs in 2008–9 plus a further £850 billion in indirect guarantees and asset protection schemes). Macroeconomic policy has been counter-productive: it has adjusted to the hollowing out of UK manufacturing and conse-quential rising balance of payments deficits not by ensuring that credit creation is directed to restoring economic competitive-ness but, perversely, by aggravating the problem. It has allowed the huge expansion of consumer credit to draw in ever more imports until equilibrium can only be restored by a significant devaluation, after which the cycle of decline continues, having been ratcheted down to a new lower level. This anti-competitive policy of cumulative decline has now reached staggering propor-tions. In 2010 the Office of Budget Responsibility (OBR) was forecasting, in the absence of growth from other sources, that household debt would rise from £1.57 trillion (115 per cent of GDP) to no less than £2.13 trillion by 2014, an increase of £56 billion or more than a third of total GDP, while at the same time bank lending to small and medium enterprises (SMEs)[62]

---

62 Calculations by the British Banking Association, Department of Business, Innovation & Skills and the Bank of England.

was persistently negative (between -3 per cent and -6 per cent each year from September 2009). This is the economic path to perdition.

(iv) From corporate tax welfare to maximising national resources
Shortage of capital for the most productive utilisation of available resources is a constraint on all growing economies. But tax avoidance (legal, but against the public interest) and tax evasion (illegal) are now on such a scale that they are no mere offence of individual greed, but rather a serious distortion of national investment and development across the world. In the UK alone it is officially admitted that the tax gap is £42 billion a year, but Richard Murphy of Tax Justice Research has estimated that the true figure may be triple that, made up of £25 billion a year in tax avoidance, £70 billion a year in tax evasion, and some £28 billion a year in outstanding debts to the tax service. Globally it has been calculated that as much as $15–20 trillion of private wealth may be hidden away in tax havens.[63]

There are several measures that could effectively address this enormous haemorrhage of capital. First, a general anti-avoidance principle (GANTIP) incorporated in UK law would allow any steps put into a transaction by a taxpayer for the sole reason of reducing their tax bill to be declared null and void by HMRC when their tax liabilities are assessed. In addition, a deterrent penalty could be levied on the taxpayer for seeking artificially to avoid their due tax responsibilities, with a similar penalty also applying to the accountants and/or lawyers who concocted the scheme for this purpose. Second, the abuse of transfer pricing

---

63   Sikka, P. and Mitchell, A., 'Let's Stop This Reverse Socialism', *Tribune*, 13 August 2010.

whereby a multinational company shifts profit in trade between companies it owns from higher-tax locations (e.g. the UK and most EU countries) to low-tax locations (e.g. Ireland, Jersey or the Cayman Islands) should be blocked by country-by-country reporting. This would require the multinational to publish its profit-and-loss account for every location in which it trades. Third, the UK's domicile rule (which allows people of foreign origin resident in the UK to be exempt from all tax on their worldwide income except that arising in the UK) should be abolished. No other country permits this loophole except Ireland. We should stop letting the UK be used by the world's mega-rich as their favourite tax haven.

Fourth, the EU Savings Tax Directive (STD) should be strengthened to include offshore trusts, the use of which is a favourite tool of the tax-cheating industry. Britain should require all its offshore secrecy jurisdictions to engage fully with automatic information exchange on a multilateral basis, starting with full co-operation with the EU STD, with the sanction that failure to do so would lead to any transaction with that jurisdiction being treated as illegal. Britain should also require all these offshore secrecy jurisdictions to place offshore company ownership on the public record, with the use of nominee directors and shareholders legally disallowed, so that the identities of those who own the company or benefit from offshore trusts are publicly disclosed. And fifth, a genuine and determined effort should be made to halt tax avoidance/evasion rather than casting a blind eye over it. As a result of intense corporate lobbying, HMRC's staff of 99,000 in 2005 was cut by a third to 68,000 in 2010, and is planned to be halved to just 56,000 by 2015, even though their work is highly cost effective, with the amount recovered per inspector ranging from 30 to 180 times the salary cost.[64] Altogether the money spent on fighting tax avoidance was halved from £3.6 billion in 2006 to just £1.9 billion in 2010. This growing shortage of HMRC resources now enables half a million companies a year to pay no tax at all by being technically dissolved and not followed up.[65]

The rigorous pursuit of all these anti-avoidance measures can be conservatively estimated to bring in additional revenues to the Treasury of at least £20 billion a year, rising over the course of a decade to some £50 billion a year. It would release a significant increase in capital availability for the revival of UK manufacturing capacity.

64   Association of Revenue and Customs, 13 August 2010.
65   Murphy, R., online pamphlet, October 2011.

CHAPTER XI

MAKING THE BANKS ACT IN THE NATIONAL INTEREST

There will be no fundamental restructuring of the British economy in the manner advocated in the last two chapters unless the role, culture and style of the banks, the cornerstone of power in UK finance capitalism, is radically changed. This requires a whole series of interconnected reforms, which are set out in this chapter.

(I) RESTRUCTURING THE BIG FIVE BANKS

The central fact about banking power in Britain today is that 85 per cent of the public's money is held by just five banks,[66] and these banks can and do use this money with little or no accountability to the public. Consequently investment in the UK economy reflects not the interests of the public or of society at large, but rather the interests of the top decision-makers in the five largest banks. Given that the total gross lending of the banking sector at £7 trillion, 507 per cent of GDP in mid-2011,[67] exceeded total government spending of £650 billion by a factor of more than ten, this tiny clique of decision-makers in these banks now commands more spending power to shape the UK economy than the whole machinery of government. This power

---

66 'The Democratic Deficit in Banking', *Positive Money*, September 2011.
67 McKinsey report on international debt, January 2012.

to create money – a power that most would assume is restricted to the Bank of England – shifted almost exclusively to private sector banks, without any parliamentary debate, as a result of successive governments failing to update legislation to take account of technological changes in banking. This now requires a series of major reforms.

The power of this dominant clique of top UK banks has to be broken up. By being 'too big to fail' they exacerbate moral hazard (i.e. the knowledge of the implicit taxpayer guarantee encourages recklessness and excessive risk-taking); they have failed in their pre-eminent task to keep adequate funding flowing to UK business; and by their size and weight in the marketplace they choke off competition and new entrants to the market. Initially that should be brought about by a 'clean break', splitting their investment from their retail arms so that underpinning by taxpayers is limited to the latter. For reasons already stated in Chapter V(1), the Vickers Commission's alternative proposal of 'Chinese walls' separating the two functions within a still integrated structure is flawed by the inevitable risk of regulatory arbitrage. However, beyond that initial break there are strong grounds in time for further disbandment of the over-dominant Big Five in order not only to pave the way for regional banks and specialist banks focused on infrastructure development, investment for a green economy, knowledge and innovation, small businesses, mortgages for low-income households etc., but above all to transform the banking culture away from its present obsession with property, overseas speculation, offshoring and tax avoidance.

(2) IMPOSING ACCOUNTABILITY ON THE FINANCE SECTOR

Accountability in finance governance, which has almost entirely dissipated in the UK, needs to be firmly re-established. The City of London was second only to Wall Street in the invention and dissemination of novel and exotic financial products (structured investment vehicles, collateralised debt obligations, credit default swaps etc.) which lay at the dark heart of the 2008 crash, yet no charges have been levelled against any bank and none of their directors prosecuted. Big finance in the neo-liberal splurge of the last decade turns out to have been big fraud. Charges against banks have abounded in other jurisdictions – the Anglo-Irish Bank over alleged fraud, the Icelandic banks over opaque deals, Lehman over its manipulated balance sheet (its notorious Repo 105s and 'debt mule' to shuffle debt around), the Swiss UBS for running 17,000 offshore accounts to evade tax, Goldman Sachs for generating a dud financial instrument packed with valueless sub-prime mortgages to enable a hedge fund client to make more than $1 billion at the expense of duped investors, to name but a few[68] – but not in the UK. Yet the scams were identical in the UK – using financial complexity to deceive, and then using so-called independent experts (lawyers, accountants, credit rating agencies, 'portfolio selection agents' etc.) to validate the deception.

In essence the big European and US banks knowingly gamed the system to expand their balance sheets ever faster and with ever lower capital ratios on the bogus claim that their lending was now much less risky. Not only did they exploit the weak Basel 2004 capital requirements to reclassify the risk of their loans and trading instruments, they even breathtakingly claimed that their new risk management techniques had so improved that the riskiness of their assets had actually halved – at a time

---

68   Hutton, W., *Observer*, 18 April 2010.

when property and share prices were breasting all-time highs! Moreover the big investment banks deliberately invented credit default swaps as an asset class to allow hedge funds to speculate against collateralised debt obligations.[69] And they gamed the regulators and investors alike, using their vast political lobbying power to create the relaxed regulatory environment to allow all this malfeasance to take place – not that Blair or Brown needed any encouragement, with the Tories urging them to go further.

Only in regulation-lite Britain has no action been taken against the bank perpetrators and their legal and accountancy accomplices. Massive fraud, deliberate deception about the value of financial assets, the use of offshoring and tax havens on an industrial scale to escape tax, widespread misselling (most recently in London, with pensions, PPI and interest rate swaps), the vast worldwide peddling of securitised assets known to be faulty, huge manipulation of balance sheets to give a false valuation of worth, conspiring with auditors and accountants to deceive the public, reckless lending or trading beyond any reasonable limits of risk – all this malpractice needs to be robustly brought to book. The cosy nexus between politics and finance has to be broken and financial malfeasance pursued with the same rigour as other organised crime.

The FSA failed to do this between 1997 and 2010, and transferring their powers back to the Bank of England, as the Tories did in 2011, will make little or no difference. Britain needs a vigorous pro-active Securities and Exchange Commission (SEC), drawing on the US model, focused on rooting out big-time financial wrongdoers. Nor is it sufficient just to hand down

---

69   Lewis, M., *The Big Short: Inside the Doomsday Machine*, Allen Lane, 2010.

a whopping fine on the bank or other financial institution or to quietly shift sideways a wrongdoing chairman or chief executive a few months after the event. The individuals guilty of financial mal-engineering on such a scale should be subject, where appropriate, to a custodial sentence and/or disqualification from any directorship/senior management position in the financial sector, either for life or for some prescribed period.

(3) REGAINING PUBLIC CONTROL OF THE MONEY SUPPLY

While there have been multiple causes of the UK breakdown and decline over the last half-century, banking policy has certainly been a primary agent. Through the shadow banking system, the proliferation of derivatives and securitisation, banks have evaded public controls and used their power ruthlessly to pursue their sectional interests. As a result of the 1971 Competition and Credit Control measures, which switched the emphasis away from quantitative controls to greater reliance on the price mechanism, followed by the 1979 abandonment of fixed exchange rates and the 1986 Big Bang and the ending of all controls over consumer credit and deregulation of housing finance, the banks seized control of the money supply. They became major generators of unsustainable asset bubbles, a source of great instability to the economy and enormous cost to taxpayers. They used their virtual monopoly (some 97 per cent) over domestic credit creation largely to feed successive property booms and speculative foreign ventures while allocating just 8 per cent to UK productive investment in the form of manufacturing, construction, communications, distribution, retail and wholesale.[70] And

---

70   Ryan-Collins, J., Greenham, T., Werner, R. and Jackson, A., *Where Does Money Come From?*, New Economics Foundation, September 2011, p. 108.

they have helped to engineer a massive misallocation of capital into tax havens which worldwide contain some £11.5 trillion of global wealth.

The case for bringing back control over the money supply into public hands is crucial for three reasons. It is needed to prevent the private banks from skewing the allocation of national funding excessively towards mortgaged property (because that has been most profitable for them, though not in the public interest). It is needed to achieve as a matter of urgent priority the rebalancing of the economy from finance to manufacturing and from the south-east to the rest of the country. And above all at a time of remorseless economic decline it is needed to ensure that the share of national resources channelled into productive investment is increased dramatically. It cannot be stressed too strongly that this is a reform of overriding strategic importance because there are no other means which will effectively secure the switch from unbridled consumerism to a framework of productive investment capable of generating a successful and sustainable manufacturing base which can securely underpin UK living standards.

There are essentially two models to secure this. One, as described in Chapter X (2) (iii), is the centralised direction of finance used (very successfully) by several Asian countries to achieve take-off after World War II, but not suited to an advanced industrial country except in extremis. The other is to bring about, through official 'guidance', the rationing of bank credit in accordance with national targets, enforced where necessary through direct quantitative controls. This was a policy which worked well in the post-war period until the 1970s, when it was steadily replaced by a purely market system based exclusively on interest rates. An adapted form of the earlier proven system should now be made the new cornerstone of monetary policy.

More generally, the powers of public institutions in credit creation and allocation need to be greatly strengthened because banking crises are usually due to credit-driven asset bubbles, and it is the role of public monetary policy to be able to prevent these. Part of that reform should also involve reviewing the restrictions on direct government credit creation imposed by the Maastricht Treaty (though there would be significant EU treaty implications here), partly because the system has been put under immense strain by the eurozone sovereign debt crisis but mainly because direct government credit creation is vitally needed, particularly to ensure that economies can be enabled to recover from deep slump.

(4) THE RESTORATION OF NECESSARY REGULATORY CONTROLS

In addition, there are a number of specific regulatory reforms which are clearly needed. Complex derivative products and other exotic financial instruments should be subjected to official inspection, and only those approved should be permitted to be traded. They should be required to pass several tests, including that they are not at risk of toxic consequences, that they are not so complex as to defy ready and accurate analysis, and that they can be shown to serve a real public interest and not merely reflect financial engineering for private gain. Anyone who attempted to circumvent the rules by going offshore or using the internet should face 'negative enforcement', i.e. their contracts would be unenforceable in law.

A reintroduction of capital controls is now widely recognised as necessary, including by the UK Treasury. Even the very conservative

Bank for International Settlements argued, in the face of global imbalances in 2005, in favour of 'reverting to a system more like that of Bretton Woods' and that 'this would only work smoothly if there were more controls on capital flows'.[71] Contrary to dismissive neo-liberal rhetoric, such controls are easily policed, as already used by governments for the purposes of anti-money-laundering measures. Thus contracts or deals made in offshore jurisdictions (or anywhere else) in defiance of financial controls can be declared void in law simply by British courts not recognising and not enforcing financial arrangements made without authorisation. The advantages would be enormous: governments would regain the power to exercise an independent monetary policy, to fix interest rates to suit the domestic economy and to preserve domestic savings for the home country, and to end the exchange rate volatility so damaging for manufacturing exports.

The financial authorities themselves recognise the need for a major rethink on economic fundamentals. A Bank of England paper released in December 2011 points out that under the Bretton Woods system (1944–71) of fixed exchange rates and capital controls, compared with the floating exchange rates and deregulated financial flows that followed after 1980, growth was higher, recessions were fewer and there were no financial crises. It notes that governments were able to pursue their domestic objectives without the constant fear of destabilising flows of hot money. The paper concludes that 'the period stands out as coinciding with remarkable financial stability and sustained high growth at the global level'.[72] In terms of trading balance

---

71   Elliott, L. et al., *A Green New Deal*, New Economics Foundation, July 2008.
72   Bank of England, Reform of the International Monetary and Financial System; Financial Stability, paper 12, December 2011.

enabling governments to deliver strong non-inflationary growth, the capacity to allocate capital efficiently and the achievement of financial stability, the paper argues that 'overall the evidence is that today's system has performed poorly against each of these three objectives, at least compared with the Bretton Woods system, with the key failure being the system's inability to maintain financial stability and minimise the incidence of disruptive sudden changes in global capital flows'.

Lastly, tax avoidance/evasion, which involves transactions of no economic substance, should be made a sub-category of money-laundering and thus treated as a criminal offence. It has been estimated that the US may be losing around $345 billion of tax revenues each year,[73] the UK over £100 billion and developing countries around $500 billion. Banks should be forbidden to provide offshore services to citizens and corporations registered onshore. To enforce this, the deposit-taking licence of banks peddling tax avoidance/evasion schemes should be withdrawn and, where appropriate, bank executives (together with accountant and lawyer associates) who have flagrantly indulged in depriving Exchequers of large-scale tax entitlements should be held personally liable to the limit of their assets for losses inflicted on taxpayers, disqualified from office and made to serve a significant custodial sentence as a deterrent to others.

---

73   US Senate Permanent Sub-Committee Investigations on the Tax Shelter Industry: the Role of Accountants, Lawyers and Financial Professionals, US Government Printing Office.

CHAPTER XII

A POSITIVE PARTNERSHIP ROLE BETWEEN STATE AND MARKETS

(I) THE GOVERNANCE OF THE NATIONAL INTEREST MODEL

The national interest business model advocated in this book will not work, however, without a major reconfiguration of the relationship between state and markets. The ideology of neo-liberal capitalism demands that the state withdraw from all but residual functions such as defence and foreign policy, and allows markets to determine all economic and social decisions. This extremist view led ultimately not only to the Great Crash of 2008–9, but also to such huge scandals as the LIBOR rate-rigging (2005–12) and the systemic corruption revealed by HSBC's money-laundering (2004–10) for drugs cartels, terrorists and pariah states. Less dramatically but more insidiously, it involved the abandonment of industrial policy, which led directly to the hollowing out of Britain's industrial base and a sharp and unsustainable rise in the UK deficit in traded goods, which reached £100 billion a year by 2010. In many areas too, as detailed later in this chapter, it led to serious private market failures and a highly dysfunctional economic structure.

Perhaps most striking of all, it failed badly even within its own terms. This is borne out in the case of the UK by the average annual growth rate by decades since the war. In the 1950s it was

2.46 per cent, in the 1960s it was 3.14 per cent, and even in the oil price-shocked and inflation-ravaged 1970s it was 2.42 per cent. Thus in the era of managed markets the broad average rate of growth was 2.7 per cent a year before the unfettered markets of neo-liberal capitalism were unleashed. In the 1980s it was 2.48 per cent, suggesting that claims of a great renaissance were overblown. In the 1990s it fell back to 2.23 per cent, and in the 2000s it fell back further to just 1.68 per cent. So across the three decades of unabashed neo-liberalism when deregulation, privatisation and market fundamentalism were applied ubiquitously, the broad average was only 2.1 per cent a year. Thus, even with the market emphasis on growth as the prime goal, leaving aside other impacts on society such as sharply rising inequality, the record of neo-liberal capitalism was poor. On that score alone there are grounds for looking to adopt a very different model.

A central characteristic of national interest capitalism is that the state–market relationship is not antagonistic or intrinsically competitive, but rather can be far more successfully developed as complementary. That makes obvious sense. The experience of the last decade demonstrates that the concept that the market is always right and that government intervention is always misplaced is simply not tenable. A more thoughtful reflection is that it's the *quality* of market operation and of government action, the *quality* of management and industrial relations, whether in the public or private sectors, that really matters. Moreover it is clear that it is this state–market model of co-operative working within an overall competitive environment that has been deployed by the most successful economies since World War II, whether Japan in its strongly expansionary MITI 1960s–1970s phase, the east Asian tiger economies of Singapore, Taiwan and Malaysia or, more recently, the new emerging BRIC world economic leaders.

Of course, there are objections frequently made to the role of both markets and the state. Markets, at least under capitalism, can be highly volatile and pro-cyclically overshoot both at the acme and nadir of cycles, which exacerbates the return to equilibrium conditions. Unemployment, regarded as the residual variable in restoring viability, is therefore subject to exaggerated swings, which are prolonged as demand evaporates at the bottom of the cycle in the absence of a compensatory expansion in public expenditure. More generally, markets depend on a steadily increasing level of demand to promote growth, since the alternative generation of credit or asset bubbles is profoundly destabilising when inevitably the bubbles implode. However, markets – again, particularly under conditions of unfettered capitalism – tend not to a uniform rise in income as the source of demand, but rather to polarisation of income and wealth; inequalities are exacerbated as the rich generally become richer and the poor poorer. In the same way, markets also lead towards a polarisation of power, as the system naturally tends towards oligopoly and the over-concentration of control in ever fewer hands. All this indicates that markets need to be carefully managed if they are not to give way to systemic instability.

Objections to the state's role in industrial policy centre around two problems. One is that government cannot understand fully what the market needs because it is too distant from it by comparison with those who participate directly and stand to gain or lose from their decisions. The other is that government is far too vulnerable to manipulation by private interests. Of course making informed decisions about interventions to create new

industries and jobs requires extensive, deep and genuine consul-
tations by government with all the main relevant interests, and of
course governments are always at risk of 'rent-seeking', corruption and capture by private interests. But that is an argument
about the manner in which government intervention should
be undertaken – that it should be an open, transparent process
with well-defined objectives – not an argument for precluding it.
When market failure is pervasive, when important markets may
contain an anti-competitive monopoly element, when market
participants may not be well informed, or when market institutions do not function as smoothly as theory claims because
of participation and transaction costs, these are weaknesses or
failures which require external intervention, and only the state
can fully perform that role.

(2) ENSURING THE INTEGRITY OF THE ECONOMIC AND INDUSTRIAL STRUCTURE

In all the major successful economies across the world since
the Second World War the government, in collaboration with
leading industrial representatives, has set out a broad strategy
which on the basis of widespread agreement can then act as
a template for bringing together other necessary elements for a
national strategy. An over-detailed economic blueprint will not
survive the volatility and unpredictability of a modern globalised
economy, but an indicative plan is essential to consolidate all the
elements in the most coherent and productive manner. Market
profit operates only at the level of the individual company; it
cannot automatically ensure the national interest is safeguarded
across the whole economic spectrum.

Britain's economic landscape has changed dramatically over
the last three decades, driven by short-term profiteering without

regard to the impacts on the effectiveness or dynamism of the residual structure as a whole. Britain has abandoned, or been forced out of, several key manufacturing sectors on the basis that the gap could be better filled by finance and services. That has proved illusory. UK car production peaked in 1972, and there is no longer any wholly British-owned mass car manufacturer. By 2010 car production contributed to only 0.7 per cent of UK economic output and involved only 0.5 per cent of total UK employment, having more than halved in the previous thirteen years – a significant loss when the Society of Motor Manufacturers and Traders (SMMT) estimates every job in the vehicle assembly line supports 7.5 elsewhere in the economy, with a supply chain worth some £5 billion annually. Shipbuilding in the UK has also shrunk drastically. The UK merchant fleet before the First World War was not only the biggest fleet in the world but accounted for 42 per cent of world tonnage. By 1938 this had reduced to 26 per cent of world tonnage, and after the war the decline accelerated from over 1 million tonnes in 1965 to 229,650 tonnes in 1993 and then to just 2,000 in 2004. Thus within less than a century UK shipbuilding fell from 42 per cent of world gross tonnage to just 0.005 per cent.

Many other British-owned industries have been laid waste. UK steel industry employment, which stood at 200,500 in 1972, fell to just 22,000 by 1999, a drop of nearly 90 per cent in less than thirty years, to a point where it accounted for less than 0.25 per cent of UK GDP and had become a smaller producer than Germany, Italy, France and Spain. UK output in the manufacture of basic metals and metal products was flat over the three decades to 2011, during which UK GDP more than doubled.[74] UK

---

74   ONS, Index of Production, and series ABMI.

manufacture of textiles and leather products has halved over the same three decades and employment has fallen by three-quarters from 600,000 in 1981 to 145,000 in 2003, a decline from 2.7 per cent to just 0.6 per cent of all UK employees over that period. Even at a time when Britain was booming, between 1997 and 2003, employment in machinery and equipment manufacture as a proportion of all employment dropped by a third, and in electrical equipment and medical instruments it also dropped by a third.

This is a saga of almost unmitigated decline across nearly the whole spectrum of UK manufacturing, driven, if not accelerated, by market fundamentalism in the absence of any long-term industrial planning. Clearly many of these industries were not internationally competitive in the face of the post-war revival of Europe and, later, the rise of the Asian tiger economies. But instead of a determined effort to restructure, advance design and innovation, increase efficiencies throughout the industrial process and improve both labour productivity and management quality, too often there was resort to the short-term expedient of quick sell-off, if not being driven into outright closure. The market did not generally act as a force for innovation, development of R&D breakthroughs or the planned concentration of resources to secure a national advantage in particular sectors or areas. The deliberate abandonment of industrial strategy during the neo-liberal era on the grounds that the market automatically knows best must rank as the biggest economic blunder in post-war history.

So how does Britain recover from this tailspin of steady industrial decline? The key issue for a turnaround in UK manufacturing is achieving competitive advantage. Michael Porter in his now-classic *Competitive Advantage of Nations*[75] argued that this derives from creating clusters of interconnected firms, suppliers, related industries and institutions, all formed in particular configurations that cannot easily be reproduced by another nation, and certainly not by a single company moving its facilities from one nation to another. Government, while not inevitably involved in such a process, can play a useful role as catalyst and challenger. It can help provide specialised factors of production, stimulate early demand for advanced products, remove distorting subsidies from non-strategic industries, and overcome failure of co-ordination when multiple private firms need to co-operate to achieve a shared goal.[76]

Such formations have been most successfully developed in the large number of internationally competitive SMEs in the *Mittelstand*, often family owned and geographically dispersed across the country, that provide the backbone of Germany's export-led manufacturing. They are supported by Germany's economic development bank (the Kreditanstalt für Wiederaufbau); the *Hausbank* system, where companies have a long-standing banking arrangement with one local bank; regional networks and chambers of commerce that provide technical support to SMEs and certify vocational training; and local economic promotion agencies, often organised as public–private partnerships.[77] A British-style version of such a system is urgently needed in the UK.

The model for successful industrial policy is clearly provided by the MITI linked business and state leadership developed

---

75   Porter, M., *The Competitive Advantage of Nations*, Free Press, 1990.
76   Greenham, T. et al., 'Why Should Government Develop an Industrial Strategy?', in *The Good Jobs Plan*, New Economics Foundation, 2010.
77   Meyer-Stamer, J. and Waltring, F. 'Behind the Myth of the Mittelstand Economy', 2000; and Venohr, B. and Meyer, K., 'The German Miracle Keeps Running', 2007.

in Japan in the 1960s and 1970s and followed by other emergent Asian economies, notably Korea, Taiwan and Malaysia as
well as, more recently, by China. Detailed and lengthy negotiation and planning are pursued in regular dialogue between
representatives of the state (ministers and relevant civil service
departments – Treasury, Industry and Trade) and business
(industry and finance) to determine key industrial and financial
priorities for the country, as well as how financial resources are to
be channelled into agreed investment priorities and which organisations are allocated logistical responsibility for implementing
each part of the overall plan. Only the state has the authority
and executive power to carry through this process, which is kept
under constant review and modified where necessary in the light
of expected outcomes and unexpected eventualities.

(3) ENSURING THE MONEY SUPPLY IS FOCUSED ON NATIONAL PRIORITIES

While Britain can boast of its wealth-creating entrepreneurs like
James Dyson, Richard Branson and Tim Waterstone, who have
built companies from scratch, they have been largely displaced by
a brash new brand of financiers and bankers who make fortunes
not by creating visionary new companies but by financially engineering existing firms' mergers, hostile takeovers, tax avoidance,
private equity and restructuring balance sheets. Thus in 2011 nearly
a fifth of the 1,000 richest persons in Britain, including fifty-one
hedge fund owners, made their money through finance while
only 11 per cent made it through industry or engineering.[78] Even
where governments have tried (rather feebly) to ensure that funding was prioritised for lending to business rather than funnelled

---

78   *Sunday Times* Rich List, May 2011.

away into consolidating bank balance sheets – Brown in 2008 as a condition for the bank bail-outs and Osborne through Operation Merlin in 2011 – the banks simply called the politicians' bluff and took the money while ignoring the quid pro quo. They even went further: in 2010 when the productive economy was being starved of cash, the banks still managed to pull together £11 billion to finance the counter-productive takeover of Cadbury by Kraft.[79]

This usurpation of the money supply by the banks for their own private ends has been widely recognised to be counter-productive. Martin Wolf, member of the 2010–11 Independent Commission on Banking, and right-wing commentator for the *Financial Times*, has observed bluntly that 'the essence of the contemporary monetary system was the creation of money, out of nothing, by private banks' often foolish lending'.[80] Through this process of unlimited credit creation the banks have inflated the money supply at a rate of 11.5 per cent a year, pushing up house prices and pricing an entire generation out of affordable accommodation while at the same time generating a mountain of personal debt. This reckless and destructive system can be broken exactly as a Tory Prime Minister did over 150 years ago. In 1844 Sir Robert Peel, noting that metal coins, the only legal form of money at that time, had been superseded by new paper notes issued by banks, took the power to create paper money away from the banks and placed it firmly under control of the Bank of England. Since then, as the technology changed, the banks have again reprivatised control of the money supply by usurping the power to create electronic money. Once again the

---

79   Lansley, S., *The Cost of Inequality: Three Decades of the Super-Rich and the Economy*, Gibson Square Books, 2011.
80   Wolf, M., *Financial Times*, 2011.

state should remove this power from the banks and make it a prerogative solely of the Bank of England.[81]

Far from this being a novel proposal it is in fact a format followed by all the most successful economies throughout the last century. Credit controls were first implemented by the German Reichsbank in 1912, then copied by the US Federal Reserve in the 1920s, and then adopted with dramatic impact by Japan in the 1940s, followed by the Korean and Taiwanese central banks and latterly in the 1980s by China. Under this so-called 'window guidance' the central bank would determine nominal GDP growth, calculate the credit creation needed to achieve this, and then allocate this credit across both banks and industrial sectors. Nor was this opposed by the banks themselves, because such a system of credit guidance offered much greater stability and increased assurance about market share and even profits. There is therefore abundant international evidence that credit guidance is an effective tool (though no guarantee that the policy goals selected will be the right ones), and when combined with both carrot and stick incentives for the banks it offers the only reliable mechanism to deliver stable (and high) economic growth that is sustainable and not plagued by recurrent banking crises. It is also a mechanism that only the state can deliver.

(4) DEALING WITH SERIOUS MARKET FAILURE

Another central role for the state, as the arbiter between conflicting interests, it to hold the ring between the demands of the markets and the claims of democracy. So far from retreating to the margins and leaving all the major decisions to be determined

---

81 The Positive Money think tank have drafted legislation that would be required to achieve this.

by market power, as neo-liberalism required, the state needs to take a robust and consistent stance on all the central principles that govern industrial, financial, social and environmental policy, within which the markets can then operate freely and flexibly. This will be strongly resisted by those who have become accustomed under the market fundamentalism of the last three decades to their economic and lobbying power triumphing for their own sectional interests, notably the City Establishment, whose well-oiled network of influence is probably unrivalled.[82] But facing down this lobbying panoply – a mixture of old boys' network, relentless campaigning and high-pressure hospitality – is essential if the state and the economy are to operate in the interests of the 99 per cent, not the 1 per cent.

Market failure is endemic throughout the private sector, and it is the role of the state to deal with these omissions, shortcomings and delinquencies in the wider national interest. One function is to ensure that the security of the nation is safeguarded. That means that the country's defence and security technology research service, which developed thermal imaging, liquid crystal displays, internet technology and other breakthroughs during the Cold War era, should be kept in public hands, not privatised as it was in 2006 under the name of Qinetiq, when sensitive defence information in private markets could readily fall into the wrong hands. Since energy security is as important in modern economies as military security, it cannot be left to the vagaries of the market, where the power companies have pocketed vast profits rather than directing them into the £200 billion investment needed to build new power stations, harness

---

82   Bureau of Investigative Journalism, *Guardian*, 10 July 2012.

renewable resources of energy (wind, wave and tidal, hydro) and effect much-improved energy saving and energy efficiency to counter the gap in the nation's energy supply widely forecast for the end of this decade. Nor is it sensible or desirable to outsource a part of the UK energy system (building a string of new nuclear stations) to a foreign power, China.[83] Rather, it is a sound reason to strengthen regulatory control of UK energy investment or to take one or more of the Big Six energy companies into public ownership to ensure that long-term energy security prevails over short-term market returns.

A second key function for the state is to counter excessive market dominance, which is both anti-competitive and against the wider public interest. There are many examples in the UK where extreme market power has been allowed to develop on the grounds that it met consumer welfare as measured by lower prices. The most extreme example is the retail sector, where 8,150 supermarket outlets now account for 97 per cent of total grocery sales, with 76 per cent sold by the four biggest retailers alone.[84] The advantage of lower prices was outbalanced by concentration, allowing dominant players to secure major insider advantages including overt and covert barriers to entry, to minimise tax liabilities, to increase returns to scale and thus force out smaller competitors, to secure greater access to capital and credit, and to achieve brand placement and opportunities for cross-subsidisation.

As a general rule no company should be permitted to control more than 10–15 per cent of market share, subject exceptionally to a case being made to the regulator that some limited

83   'Beijing in talks with UK government to invest billions to build 5 nuclear reactors', *Guardian*, 21 July 2012.

84   Blond, P., 'Welfare killed the competition', *New Statesman*, 30 January 2012.

extension be granted on demonstrably wider public interest grounds. That would require a new regulatory framework. A new Competition and Takeover Commission would regulate against excessive market share, ensure that takeovers did not breach wider UK public interests, and aim to shift the balance of interest more towards employees, shareholders and stakeholders. An Accountancy and Audit Commission would have the brief to control creative accountancy, off-balance-sheet activity and collusion between auditors and executives.[85] And an Insolvency Commission would operate a US-style Chapter 11 bankruptcy provision to place the emphasis on restructuring and survival rather than closure and dismantling.

Third, there is a clear need for the state to engender an atmosphere of trust and morality in the corporate sector and to re-establish the principle of accountability to the public inter-est, which is almost universally perceived to have been lost. The roll-call of corporate malfeasance over the last decade has been extensive and has involved the biggest names. HSBC laundered billions of dollars for drug cartels, terrorists and pariah states in a 'pervasively polluted' culture that persisted for years.[86] Barclays, and perhaps another fourteen major banks worldwide, stand accused of the massive LIBOR interest rate-fixing scandal during 2005–10, both to enhance their own trading profits and to give a falsely optimistic impression of the banks' strength in the aftermath of the global crash, thus manipulating through LIBOR some $800 trillion-worth of financial instruments.[87] BAE, Britain's biggest arms manufacturer, was pursued by the

---

85   Sikka, P., 'Carry On Casino Banking', *Chartist*, November 2011.
86   US Senate committee report, July 2012.
87   *The Economist*, 7 July 2012, p. 13.

Serious Fraud Office over alleged £1.2 billion bribes to the son of the Saudi Defence Minister to secure a £43 billion arms order in 1985.

Again, more than 100 British construction firms, including Balfour Beatty, were found guilty in September 2009 of illegal price-fixing, especially the use of artificially high cover pricing by a competitor acting in collusion to gain a contract.[88] The Royal Mail secretly punted £5 billion of its pension fund into an off-balance-sheet vehicle in 2009 to place highly risky bets on financial derivatives on the Stock Exchange, behaving 'like a hedge fund that happens to deliver letters'.[89] The EU Competition Commissioner found that big pharma, possibly including GSK, had spent nearly £200 million to block the marketing of cheaper generic drugs to preserve their own profits while making patients pay more. Innospec, a UK firm in Cheshire which manufactured tetraethyl lead as a fuel additive until it was banned in the US and Europe, then paid $5 million in bribes to Iraqi officials between 2001 and 2008 to continue the sale of this poisonous chemical in poorer countries as well as bribing the same officials to fail the field test of an alternative, safer product.[90] And so on and so on – the list is a very long one and reflects the 'anything goes', 'get what you can', 'no questions asked' mentality of the neo-liberal era.

Yet in the decade to 2009 only two persons in the UK were prosecuted under an international bribery convention, compared with eighty-eight in the US, twenty-six in Germany and forty in Italy.[91] This laxity, fed by the myth that the UK somehow stands

88 *Guardian*, 23 September 2009.
89 *Guardian*, 24 September 2010.
90 *Guardian*, 10 August 2010.
91 *The Economist*, 2 April 2011.

for probity and fair play, will only be disabused when three reforms are instituted. A powerful and fiercely independent Justice Department, transparently at arm's length from the government, has to be prepared to take on the biggest corporations where necessary. Gross offences as outlined here will only be effectively deterred if, in addition to huge fines on the company paid for by the shareholders, the relevant directors themselves are subjected to loss of limited liability and forced to contribute to the limit of their assets as well as being, where appropriate, much more likely to face a long prison sentence. Third, the state must ensure much stronger protections are put in place to safeguard whistle-blowers, the best source of the truth about abuses that would otherwise be covered up, against intimidation or harassment.

(5) REDRAWING THE PUBLIC SECTOR–PRIVATE SECTOR BOUNDARIES

A further major role for the state is to define the balance between the public and private sectors and to establish how they can best co-operate with each other in the wider national interest. Where the private sector is dynamic and innovative, as entrepreneurial capitalism is meant to be, the state should offer every assistance it can to enable it to thrive. Where, however, it is patently inefficient, losing market share, being displaced by imports, or not responding to technological change or other external pressures, and where this is occurring in sectors important to the overall economy, the state has to intervene and create the conditions for change.

There can be little question that outsourcing was taken to absurd lengths under the neo-liberal regime. This was most starkly illustrated by the spectacular failure in July 2012 of the UK-based G4S, the world's largest security firm, to provide even half of the guards stipulated under its huge £284 million Olympics contract, a degree of incompetence so great that it will finally bury the fantasy that private companies are always more efficient. Even the former Thatcher minister William Waldegrave warned Conservatives never to 'make the mistake of falling in love with free enterprise', adding that people who believe 'private companies are always more efficient than the public service have never worked in real private enterprise'.[92] Jeremy Hunt, then Culture Secretary, confirmed this by admitting, with disarming frankness, that it's 'absolutely normal' that private contractors fail to deliver.

Indeed, while G4S is the most egregious example, it is only the latest in a stream of recent outsourcing scandals. These include the alleged fraud, incompetence and inefficient operation of the huge A4E welfare-to-work contract, the colossal losses made by Somerset Council in a joint private sector debacle, the estimated £25 billion wasted on PFI schemes over and above the cost if the government had undertaken them directly, the more than doubling of public subsidies to £5.4 billion a year caused by rail privatisation and fragmentation, and the water shortage in rain-sodden southern England in the summer of 2012 brought about by a privatised water company which had sold off twenty-five reservoirs over the previous twenty years to make huge profits and distribute £5 billion in dividends to shareholders.[93]

The grounds for reversing these disastrous mistakes are not only that they are hugely wasteful to the public purse, but also that they represent a parasitic operation, not a genuine increment to public value. They creatively manufacture profit from

92   Waldegrave, W., *The Times*, 17 July 2012.
93   Milne, S., *Guardian*, 18 July 2012.

existing provision rather than produce new goods and services. The record of outsourcing and privatisation is that it regularly reduces service quality while not delivering on promised savings. Even where it does make some savings, it is almost always at the expense of the pay and conditions of low-paid workers, despite the supposed TUPE safeguards, which are elaborately circumvented. At the same time the public service ethos is undermined, the professionalism and morale of key employees eroded, administration and transaction costs inflated and public accountability lost. Worst of all, the privateering companies that win these contracts, despite the rhetoric, don't have specialist skills at all, but often are simply conglomerates which have established networks of political influence and have learnt the insider rules for winning contracts.

PFI schemes in particular, which will otherwise cost the taxpayer the gigantic sum of £301 billion over the next fifty years, should be ended wherever possible. The PFI concept rests on three central premises: that it allows the government to commission services it wouldn't otherwise be able to afford, that the private sector is more efficient than the public sector and that private companies can run public services more cheaply than the state could. Each of these claims is false. The healthy surplus in the public finances in the Blair–Brown decade to 2007 did not necessitate resort to PFI at all. A *British Medical Journal* analysis of May 2002 found that the government's own figures showed that before 'risk' was taken into account, new hospital schemes would have been built far more cheaply with public funds, but when 'transferred risks' were factored in, the comparison miraculously favoured PFI, in several cases by less than 0.1 per cent. And private companies' performance was systematically rigged by permitting them to use discount rates wholly out of line with inflation, allowing VAT to be reclaimed (but not on publicly backed schemes), exempting them from the 6 per cent 'capital charge' on buildings they owned (but payable by public authorities), and offering them an 11 per cent annual Treasury grant (for PFI schemes but not for publicly funded projects). This gigantic corporate welfare gravy train, the neo-liberal ideal of a fully privatised corporate state, should be terminated, with existing contracts paid off by forfeiture where conditional targets have not been met and by carefully targeted tax levies focused to the extent feasible on the beneficiaries.

Finally, there are areas within the economy where the private sector has clearly failed and where a range of alternative models could be better deployed in the public interest. Most obviously in banking: RBS and Lloyds should be retained in the public sector but broken up to serve specific domestic remits, while the disgraced HSBC and Barclays should be taken over and simi-larly given new management and very different public goals.

House-building has been a colossal failure over the last two decades, with 1.8 million households on council waiting lists and 80,000–100,000 homeless, yet local authority social housing completions fell from 16,380 a year in 1990 to just 260 in 2007,[94] and housing starts in 2012 were at their lowest peace-time level since 1923 and still falling. A public house-building service is clearly needed both to increase dramatically the overall number of houses built and, above all, to increase the supply of social housing and of affordable accommodation for first-time buyers.

Energy supply in the hands of Big Six oligopoly has not only

---

94   DCLG figures from www.communities.gov.uk/documents/housing/xls/1473507.xls

failed to put in hand the necessary long-term investment the nation needs, but has also manipulated domestic markets against the interests of consumers, especially the 5–6 million fuel poor, by exploiting the hidden interplay between wholesale and retail contracts, bamboozling consumers with 300 complex tariffs, and still (according to OFGEM after eighteen reviews of the energy market since 2001) not providing honest figures of what they are paying for power. One or more of the energy companies should be brought into public ownership to ensure long-term investment is guaranteed and that effective regulation can be applied in the light of the true figures to protect UK consumers.

Similarly, renationalisation of rail, supported by 95 per cent in a poll of Londoners in 2009, would reintegrate the badly fragmented national network, improve rail safety, strengthen the modal switch to public transport, reduce regulatory bureaucracy and reduce public subsidies to train companies by nearly two-thirds. The McNulty report of May 2011 found that so great are the inefficiencies of fragmentation (and the dividend and profit take-off) in the UK that train fares were 30 per cent higher in this country than in France, Holland, Sweden and Switzerland, yet UK operating costs were 40 per cent higher than in those countries. Single national control of rail, as exists in most other countries, could be achieved at minimal cost by not renewing existing franchises, taking back franchises where standard requirements are not met, disallowing premature discharge of franchises without penalty, and perhaps a windfall tax on the excess profits of rolling stock companies.

One last example – and there are many others – concerns the big welfare-to-work companies (mainly A4E, Serco and Reed) which have been awarded huge government contracts of

£3–5 billion yet have been found to fall dismally short of their contract targets – against 30–50 per cent back-to-work targets achieving no better than 13–16 per cent. Even those they 'successfully' got back into work were soon out of work again, a quarter within three months. Any serious labour market policy for training and job placement requires a great deal more commitment than these crude 'carrot and stick' programmes. Significantly, the cross-party Commons Public Accounts Committee found the public sector Jobcentre Plus to be more efficient and effective than the private providers, even though the latter creamed off the easier claimants whereas more problematic groups like the mentally ill, ex-prisoners or addicts were palmed off to the public or voluntary providers.

CHAPTER XIII

FLATTENING INEQUALITY AND RAISING THE LEVEL OF DEMAND

(I) THE GOAL OF STEADY GROWTH IN OVERALL DEMAND

The previous five chapters have spelt out the essential reforms required to establish a new business model to replace the total breakdown of neo-liberal capitalism: a more constructive policy in the immediate term to confront the deficit and restore growth; the central focus on a major revival of manufacturing to underpin living standards and pre-empt a slide into ever deeper trading deficits; a rebalancing of the economy away from over-domination by a luxuried elite towards emphasis on productive investment; ending bank excesses and restoring their real role of servicing the domestic economy; and re-establishing a strong partnership role of interdependence between state and markets.

That still leaves one crucial element unresolved, as noted in Chapter VIII (4), which ultimately was a major factor in the downfall of the whole neo-liberal model: how is an adequate level of aggregate demand to be generated without resort to the creation of household credit or a housing or any other asset bubble which eventually will implode disastrously? In the last three decades the average price of UK housing was inflated in real terms by 82 per cent in the decade to 1989, then crashed, and then was inflated again by a further three times as much (a real-terms rise of 245 per cent) in the decade to 2006[95] before crashing again in the 2007–9 collapse. Household borrowing reached £1.45 trillion in 2010–11, equal to Britain's entire GDP, largely for mortgages but also one-seventh for credit cards, and while disposable income and GDP grew slightly over 50 per cent during 2000–08, financial assets grew four times faster, with an increase of 220 per cent.[96] For sustainable growth there cannot be a return to this helter-skelter volatility and asset inflation and destruction.

Sustainable demand is broadly dependent on consumer expenditure and exports, the former optimised by near-full employment and greater income equality and the latter by trading competitiveness. The neo-liberal capitalism of the last three decades, however, significantly squeezed the wage share in GDP, pushed unemployment generally to the 2.5–3.0 million level, and enormously extended inequality. By contrast, a capitalism that genuinely served the national interest would make near-full employment (within the 0.5–1.0 million unemployment range) and a rebalanced share of GDP between wages and profits (from the current 53 per cent wage share much closer to the pre-1980s 65 per cent share) into central objectives of economic policy.

That would generate a much steadier growth in demand. Under neo-liberalism, however, the share of income taken by the top 1 per cent of earners doubled from 7.1 per cent in 1970 to 14.3 per cent in 2005, while for the top 0.1 per cent it rose to 5 per cent.[97] For the poorest tenth it slipped to just 3 per cent. Since poorer households have a much higher propensity to spend

95   Nationwide Building Society.
96   Bank of International Settlements, report 2010, p. 28.
97   OECD, 'Divided We Stand' report, 2011.

than the super-rich, reversing the huge ballooning of inequality since 1980 would substantially make for a more stable growth of demand. The mechanisms to achieve this are examined in the rest of this chapter.

(2) ELIMINATING UNACCEPTABLE INEQUALITY

As spelt out in Chapter II (2), the poor – the seventh of all UK families living below the poverty line of 60 per cent of median earnings – grew hardly better off at all even in the boom years of 1984–89 and 1994–2007, and after the financial crash and imposed austerity are likely to suffer a decade or more (2007–20) of sharply declining living standards. The rich, and particularly the 1 per cent super-rich, managed to pump up both their income and wealth, in many cases to stratospheric levels. Chapter II also showed that neither of the two arguments used to justify this polarisation – that excessive rewards reflected exceptional wealth creation and that wealth at the top doesn't harm anybody else – stands up to even the slightest scrutiny.

So what should be done to produce a system of rewards that is fair and defensible at all levels of the income distribution? A High Pay Commission has been advocated on the grounds that that is where the grossest excesses have occurred. But it has the drawback of artificially imposing or recommending relatively rigid guidelines on types of work that are often highly discrete and heterogeneous, where appropriate rewards can only be properly settled organically within the organisation as a whole. It also fails to tackle the fundamental framework driving up extreme inequality, namely that manual workers' pay is largely determined by national pay bargaining, white-collar pay depends on individual contracts laid down by the employer, and boardroom pay at the top is settled secretly by the chairman's own chosen remuneration committee, whose members engage in mutual back-scratching in determining each other's salary and multiple incentive schemes.

Far better, therefore, would be the introduction of whole-company pay bargaining, basing pay awards across the whole range of occupations on job evaluation and performance rating by those with direct knowledge and experience working collectively within the organisation. Representatives of all the main grades within the enterprise would meet at least once a year and review the current financial position in terms of depreciation, debt, stock provision, dividends, investment, cash flow etc., and on that basis determine the funding availability for pay increases throughout the whole organisation for the next year. Each representative of each group would make the case for a certain pay increase for their own group. What was finally awarded to each group would depend on the decision of all the other representatives jointly, subject to the obvious proviso that the more that was allotted to one group, the less would be available for others.

Such a framework for determining pay has substantial merits. Instead of the selfish pursuit of sectional interests by each group regardless of the welfare of the organisation overall, it would require each group to relate its own interests to those of others and to the enterprise as a whole. Instead of pay deals being cooked up in smoke-filled rooms or in private negotiations behind closed doors, the whole process would be transparent. Instead of pay being seen as spoils to be maximised in a constant market struggle, it would for the first time be seen as an expression of relative worth, to be explained and argued for publicly. Above all, instead of pay being seen as an instrument of power exerted by leaders over all the subordinate groups within their organisations, it becomes a joint decision for those groups themselves, a decentralisation of power among those directly affected, though firmly subject to all the necessary economic realities.

Such a system would operate to maintain inequalities, but no more than those that could be rationally justified. If the enterprise was to succeed, those with needed scarce skills would still have to be bid for at a premium within an open market system. But the pressure from below to maximise incentives throughout the organisation and not only in the higher reaches would mean that any special pleading would be restrained to the minimum strictly necessary. Over much of the middle stratum pay is quite finely calibrated to match market signals, reflecting differential skills. However, at the base of the pay hierarchy whole-company pay bargaining is unlikely to end wage poverty by itself, and additional measures would be necessary to eliminate it.

(3) ENDING POVERTY PAY

According to the Department of Work and Pensions' (DWP) definition, any family living on less than 60 per cent of median household earnings after housing costs – £214 a week in 2011/12[98] – is deemed to be living in poverty. About a fifth of all employees in the UK, over five million people, earn below this level, and altogether 13.4 million people in the UK live in these poverty households. The national minimum wage, at £6.08 per hour in 2011/12, is currently set slightly above this level at £228 a week. However, the principle of a living wage, fixed at some £7–7.50 an hour, was negotiated across a hundred organisations

---

98   Hansard, 8 June 2011, and the 'Households Below Average Income' report on the DWP website.

in London in 2009/10, and the similar concept of a minimum income standard (MIS) was developed by the Joseph Rowntree Foundation.

The calculation is based on the minimum income needed by a family or individual to ensure good health, adequate child development and social inclusion. The 2009 MIS report concluded that even a single person with no dependants living in council housing needs at least £13,900 a year before tax to afford a basic but acceptable standard of living. That would amount to about £267 a week or £7.09 an hour. The MIS project produced other figures to show that the majority of UK families would need to have two adults working full time, each earning £7.14 an hour, to provide a basic but adequate living standard. But about 4.85 million adults, about one in five of all employees, were paid less than £7.19 per hour in 2009. A quarter of those worked in the public sector, two-thirds were women, and a half were part-time workers.

On this basis, ending poverty wages in terms of ensuring that all employees secure a basic but adequate standard of living would require by 2012 that no wages be paid at less than £7.50 an hour, and that this be increased each year at least in line with average earnings and enforced by a sufficient number of wages inspectors with deterrent penalties against cheating employers. The usual objections are that it would be inflationary, cause unemployment and undermine efficiency. In fact, if it were introduced in the second half of this decade when the economic recovery is likely still to be subdued, it would not be inflationary, especially if the increase were phased in over a two-to-three-year period. Nor would it increase unemployment, judging by international experience in such countries as France, the Netherlands and Belgium, where the minimum wage is higher yet they do not report any rise in joblessness on that count. Indeed, a higher minimum wage can actually increase overall employment by raising the level of total demand, which should generate jobs elsewhere in the economy, exactly the objective sought earlier for macroeconomic reasons.

On sapping efficiency, again the objections are the reverse of the truth. Industries which come to rely on cheap labour provide a way by which inefficient producers and obsolete technologies can compete: they can force down wages and conditions of work in order to survive. Competition should be based on quality of product, design or productive efficiency. Low pay imposes economic costs in terms of technological backwardness, reduced productivity and lower standards of service to the consumer. If low wages are necessary to the British economy (compared, say, with the German economy), it doesn't show how well the market is working; it shows how badly it's working.

(4) REVERSING POVERTY IN RETIREMENT

Whole-company pay bargaining plus a higher and steadily increasing minimum wage should not only raise the level of aggregate demand as a necessary macroeconomic condition for greater long-term stability but should also, over time, squeeze out unacceptable inequality at work. However, that still leaves unacceptable inequality in retirement, where about a fifth of all pensioners remain in relative poverty under the DWP definition. UK pensions are among the worst in western Europe, across both the public and private sectors. In the public sector in 2009–10, according to the Hutton review, a typical local government worker received a pension of just £77 a week, a civil

servant £119 a week and a teacher £188 a week, the first two
falling well below the poverty line. In the private sector 10–15
million workers have no occupational pension at all, final salary
schemes have been almost wholly phased out and the remaining
defined contribution schemes and private pensions are dependent on stock market returns, which have declined in the last
decade, with pension contributions by employers having halved
in recent years and payouts fallen by as much as two-thirds.
This is an area of massive market failure where inequality has
ballooned even more egregiously than in employment: FTSE
100 directors get an average pension of £3.4 million (£65,385
a week) by comparison with a state pension of around £140 a
week, i.e. 467 times as much.

The private sector pensions market is indelibly scarred with
overdependence on stock market volatility, very high administrative transaction costs (20–40 per cent), repeated misselling
scams, employer manipulation of contributions, dependence on
tax relief and subsidies, and above all a whole working career of
employee contributions yielding pensions that are in most cases
still below the poverty line, requiring means-tested top-ups by
the state. The only effective way to eliminate poverty and excessive inequality in retirement is through a new comprehensive
state insurance pension scheme which is pitched at a level that
ensures that everyone at the end of their working lives receives
a pension as of right which guarantees at minimum a basic but
acceptable standard of living well above the official DWP 60 per
cent-of-median-earnings poverty line, and for the vast majority
a high-quality pension that offers a comfortable lifestyle.

There are several key components of such a scheme. It would
build on top of the basic state pension, upgraded each year in

line with average earnings, an upper tier where contributions would be income related and subsequent pension payouts similarly linked, though with a mild redistributive tilt in favour of the lower paid. It would be introduced gradually over a ten-year period in order that the extra contributions could be managed at an acceptable level. While all employees would be required to contribute to underwrite the guaranteed minimum (basic plus income-related top-up) scheme, anybody would be free to opt out of contributions above this level so long as they could show it would produce a pension above the guaranteed minimum pension (GMP) level.

The overall scheme would be buttressed by a near-full employment policy (which a rebalancing of the economy and a major revival of manufacturing would steadily over time produce) and by a significant increase in contributions produced by a higher minimum wage (as proposed above), and would itself contribute through higher pensions to raising aggregate demand within the economy. It would also end the demeaning necessity for two million of the poorest pensioners to seek means-tested benefits, which at present a third of those entitled find either too degrading or too difficult to manage even to claim. It would finally end deep and extensive pensioner poverty, which remains one of the worst, though largely ignored, perennial scandals in Britain today.

(5) REVERSING THE TAX AVOIDANCE DRAIN

Generating a fairer income reward system, raising the lowest pay and consolidating pension payments well above the means-tested poverty line, all of which have hitherto been missing, will together significantly enhance the level of aggregate demand within the economy. The other major element that has been missing from available national resources and thus the buttressing of overall demand is a fair tax contribution from the mega-rich. There are three main reasons for this. First, because of their political lobbying power they have been subject to much milder tax levies, relative to their extreme income and wealth, than the rest of the population. Second, they have largely circumvented the income tax rules which regulate the income of everyone else by switching the great majority of their remuneration into share options, massive share allocations, 'incentive plans' paid in practice irrespective of performance, so-called fringe benefits and enormous bonuses. Third, and by far the most significantly, they employ a retinue of City lawyers and accountants to squirrel their assets away into tax havens and to circumvent every new Treasury statute devised to stop them.

The scale of tax avoidance/evasion today is staggering. According to the latest study by the chief economist at the McKinsey consultancy, the global super-rich had at least £13 trillion ($21 trillion) hidden in tax havens by the end of 2010, a sum equal to the size of the US and Japanese economies combined.[99] The report also found that the fifty leading banks worldwide managed more than $12.1 trillion in cross-border invested assets for private clients, above all UBS, Credit Suisse and Goldman Sachs. It also estimated that fewer than 100,000 persons worldwide own about $9.8 trillion of the wealth held offshore. Nearly half of the total £13 trillion is held in British Crown Dependencies and Offshore Territories. The potential for tracking down large portions of this offshore wealth and bringing it back into circulation is enormous. But can it be done?

---

99   Henry, J., 'The Price of Offshore Revisited', Tax Justice Network, July 2012.

There is a whole range of measures which can be taken, but have been deliberately played down because of collusion between the political class and the bankers (who provide half of annual donations each year to the Tory Party). Treasury figures estimated tax avoidance by UK citizens at £42 billion in 2009, with a total of £228 billion over the six years to 2010. The annual average figure is equivalent to about a third of the entire UK deficit. It matters because the loss of it entails either much lower public expenditure than would otherwise be the case or much higher taxes on the other 99 per cent of the population to compensate.

Five measures, none so far even attempted, could fundamentally change the prospects for jobs and growth if £40 billion a year, or a big part of it, were brought back into circulation. First, government could pass a GANTIP (general anti-tax avoidance principle) law whereby any scheme whose primary purpose is artificial contrivance to avoid tax, rather than any genuine economic transaction, could be declared null and void by HMRC. Not only would the tax avoidance be blocked, but an additional levy of three to five times that amount should be imposed as a deterrent penalty for seeking wilfully to sidestep the will of parliamentary statute, with a similar penalty for any lawyers or accountants who were partners in the transgression.

Second, government should seek a new international financial standard which requires country-by-country reporting by transnational corporations (TNCs). The aim of this is to close the colossal loophole of transfer pricing. These huge companies make profits in the UK or other relatively high-tax developed countries, but for tax purposes claim to be resident in the Caymans, Bahamas, Bermuda and other offshore boltholes where they do little or no business, booking large chunks of their profits there while deducting interest-bearing debt and other costs in the UK, thus ending up paying little or no tax at all in the UK. A National Audit Office report in 2007 found that, despite record profits, 220 of the 700 biggest companies paid no corporation tax whatever and a further 210 companies each paid less than £10 million. Google, for example, which dominates the internet, with revenues from the UK soaring to £6.3 billion over six years, has paid only some £8 million (0.12 per cent) in corporation tax. If all off-balance-sheet structures were required to be brought back onto the books, that measure plus country-by-country reporting, which crucially would disclose trading data for both third party and intra-group transactions, would shatter the secrecy of tax havens across the world, expose the workings of hedge funds and private equity operators, and end much of the recent abusive securitisation, as well as putting a stop to most transfer pricing.

There are other measures too which could be readily taken. The EU Savings Tax Directive, which the UK government has repeatedly tried to water down, should be strengthened to include offshore trusts, a favourite tool of the tax-cheating industry. The non-dom. rule should be abolished, since it attracts many dubious characters from abroad whose contribution to the UK is nil or very little, but who do invest heavily in property and substantially inflate house prices. And if the political will were there, the UK tax havens could be closed down. The UK Crown Dependencies hold $7 trillion of US bank deposits and probably enable £30 billion of tax-dodging by UK citizens. The Cayman Islands alone have only 30,000 inhabitants but no fewer than 457,000 (shell) companies. Their activities could be quickly ended if the UK government enforced the rule that unless they provided full and automatic information on all such funds held by them which could then be taxed, any transactions with such tax havens would be declared illegal.

(6) TAX THE SUPER-RICH!

One final means by which the level of aggregate demand could be substantially enhanced would be to make the hyper-rich pay a fair and progressive tax contribution on their income and wealth. HMRC figures show that, compared with UK median pay of £440 a week, the highest-paid 1 per cent (about 300,000 persons) have an income of more than £3,000 a week, while the top 0.5 per cent take £5,200 a week and the top 0.1 per cent take £22,700 a week. The average pay of chief executives of FTSE companies is now £92,300 a week. However, as a result of extensive tax reliefs, particularly higher-rate pension tax relief, and numerous devices to convert high income into less taxed capital or through outright offshoring of remuneration, they pay far less in tax than their overall income would suggest – indeed, as one financier wryly observed, many private equity partners pay less tax than their cleaning ladies. This should be blocked by requiring all extremely rich persons to pay 32–40 per cent of all their gross income in whatever form it is held.

The figures on wealth are even more dramatic. The *Sunday Times* Rich List shows that the richest 1,000 persons in Britain, just 0.003 per cent of the population, had assets of £414 billion in 2012 and had increased their wealth by no less than £155 billion in the three previous years of austerity (for everyone else). The richest 100 within this group included seventy-seven billionaires, the other twenty-three owning over £750 million each. Just below this topmost layer of wealth, the richest 1 per cent hold assets of about £800 billion, while the richest 10 per cent (around three million people) own £4 trillion, nearly half of total UK personal wealth. Any fair and comprehensive tax system would bring these colossal sums into the tax net if there were to be any sense of equity and balance of responsibility between poor and rich.

In the UK there is currently no wealth tax, and even the capital gains tax rate has been reduced to 28 per cent. One proposal targeted to meet Britain's immediate financial crisis is that since the richest 10 per cent own wealth equal to five times the UK entire accumulated national debt, a one-off wealth tax levied at 20 per cent could wipe off this debt and thus lay the foundations for restoring demand, investment and growth.[100] A more long-term plan to achieve a sustainable rise in the level of demand would be to tax the asset gains on an annual basis and use the proceeds for productive investment and job creation. Thus taxing the gains of the richest 1,000 individuals over the last three years at the current capital gains tax rate of 28 per cent would (potentially) yield £43 billion, enough without any increase at all in public borrowing to generate 1–1.5 million jobs over the next two to three years. If that same tax plan were applied to the richest 1–2 per cent, the positive impact in bringing dormant capital into entrepreneurial use, raising economic growth and sharply cutting the dole queues would be all the greater.

At this point, now that these last six chapters have set out a detailed framework for a very different, more productive, balanced and sustainable business model for the economy, the question obviously arises: how will that model impact upon, and equally be influenced by, Britain's social hierarchy, power structure and values system? The next four chapters aim to answer that question.

---

100 Philo, G., Glasgow Media Group.

PART 4

HOW NATIONAL INTEREST CAPITALISM WOULD RADICALLY TRANSFORM BRITAIN'S SOCIETY AND CULTURE

CHAPTER XIV

CLASS AND SOCIAL MOBILITY

The formative principles of neo-liberal capitalism have moulded not only the economy, via unfettered freedom for markets, privatisation and deregulation, but also industry and commerce, via the promotion of hegemonic corporate power and the suppression of the unions as well as society via an enormous expansion of inequality. The formative principles of national interest capitalism, on the other hand, are not limited to the achievement of financial stability via banking reform and public guidance in capital allocation, an activist role for the state in resuscitating manufacturing industry and controlling market cyclical excesses, a non-antagonistic relationship between the public and private sectors based on complementary role requirements, and international adjustment via some capital controls and joint obligations for both debtor and creditor countries.

They also require a more equal income distribution and full employment to secure the steady growth of aggregate demand; a stakeholder partnership between management and unions in industry to enable a greater empowerment of people in their working lives; the reduction of class barriers to achieve a real equality of opportunity for all; a much stronger framework of accountability to afford citizens more effective redress against the abuse of power; and the promotion of the values of community, inclusiveness and mutuality in society. The following four chapters set out how these latter objectives should be implemented.

(I) BREAKING DOWN THE UK'S RIGID CLASS BARRIERS FROM THE EARLIEST AGE

Redressing the profound discrimination that holds so many millions back in Britain in the most deeply embedded class culture in Europe, as set out in Chapter II, is a daunting task requiring co-ordinated and systematic action on several interrelated fronts. This discrimination is driven not only by income and wealth inequalities, but also by occupational separateness, huge educational disparities, ideological prejudice, cultural apartheid and vastly differential aspiration. Combining all the necessary reforms will involve large initial outlays but will achieve overall substantial long-term economic savings as well as proving socially transformative.

Class divisions start very early in life and require equally early interventions if their long-term impact on later life chances is to be averted. Convincing evidence shows that early experiences such as the quality of the home environment, family structure, pre-school care and relationships with caring adults produce a pattern of development in later life that is hard to reverse even through schooling. That has already been modestly tackled: Education Action Zones in 1998 poured extra funds into education in poor areas, Sure Start in 1999 helped poor families with everything from breastfeeding support to baby massage, and from 2004 all pre-school children aged at least three years were entitled to some free nursery care. Yet although £21 billion was spent on new schemes for pre-school children in the decade to

2007,[101] the gap in attainment between rich and poor children remained as wide as ever, either because the care was of dubious quality or because the offer of help was more enthusiastically taken up by middle-class families living nearby.

A US programme, the Harlem Children's Zone (HCZ), suggests that piecemeal approaches will never deliver real change for those at the bottom. Geoffrey Canada, the founder of the project, noted that the latest research on the brain showed that much of a child's capacity to think and to learn was set in the first three years of life. Middle-class families spent those years talking, singing and reading to their children. Poor children, however, arrived at school with an average of twenty-five hours of one-to-one reading behind them, while middle-class children had 1,700 hours and their vocabulary was twice as large. They had learnt to argue and discuss, had been introduced to conceptual thinking, and above all had confidence. By the age of three they had heard six times as many encouraging words as discouraging ones, but poor children had been reprimanded two to three times more than they had been praised.

Canada, with extraordinary ambition, sought to reverse this differential at root with an intense programme starting before birth, with parenting classes transforming adults' approach to their babies, and continuing until after college. It involved pre-kindergartens, tutoring, dance and sport classes, food co-ops, social service, and housing and health aid, with every child in the zone being offered support. At a total cost of $5,000 a child per year HCZ produced revolutionary results. With the schools' intake random and very deprived (10 per cent of the children

---

101   *The Economist*, 1 September 2007, p. 26.

lived in homeless shelters or foster care), a Harvard University evaluation of the project found that the combination of community transformation, high-quality teaching and parental support was 'enormously effective at raising the achievement level of the poorest minority children'. Previously just 7 per cent of black fourteen-year-olds passed their grade in maths, but HCZ staggeringly produced 97 per cent of eighth-graders performing at or above grade level. The Harvard study concluded that HCZ vastly exceeded the effects of all other initiatives like lowering class size, offering bonuses for teachers in tough schools, or running classic early childhood programmes like Head Start. It is true the price was high, with one teacher per four children in the kindergarten and half the teachers leaving the schools at the end of the first year because they were not suited to the job, but the rewards were astonishing.[102]

The key lesson from HCZ is that the breakthrough in overcoming entrenched class (and in this case also racial) barriers requires systematically raising the aspirations of a whole community simultaneously so that going to college and avoiding drugs or teenage pregnancy becomes normal behaviour. Just focusing on a minority of promising children won't achieve the prize of transformation; only if a critical mass (at least half) can be incentivised to become ambitious and hard-working, with support from an adult, do the counter-pressures of alienation and resistance begin to drop away. This is a seminal experiment which really worked in the most inhospitable conditions. Similar experiments should be launched in the UK among Britain's most difficult and hardened communities and if the results are equally

102 Russell, J., *Guardian*, 6 August 2009.

dramatic, they should be rolled out where necessary across the whole country. It could be largely funded by the phasing out of existing schemes that have proved much less successful.

(2) ENDING SELECTIVE CLASS DIVISIONS IN EDUCATION

While this approach for confronting the foundations of class apartheid in Britain is fundamental, there are several reforms that need to be built on it to remove the social, psychological and institutional mechanisms that intensify class hierarchy. By far the most important measure is reforming the structure, goals and values of the educational system. To a degree unique across the Western world, education in England is riven by the fundamental divide between the private and state schools, which structures every aspect of the economic, political and social culture in later life in a manner that concentrates wealth, advantage and power on the scions of the richest families, but at huge inhibition to the talents of and opportunities for the rest of the population. The 2007 report by the Office for Fair Access (OFFA) found that the link between background and attainment was already evident at just twenty-two months, but schooling widens the gap substantially.

At GCSE the children of higher professionals get good grades nearly three times more than children of manual workers. Fewer working-class children take A levels and those that do get lower scores, while pupils at private schools (7 per cent of the national cohort) account for 15 per cent of entries but take about 30 per cent of A grades. Class factors then reinforce this lopsided access to privilege even further. Even those children from poorer homes who do well are less likely to apply to the top universities. OFFA has estimated, on the basis of grades alone, that some 4,500 state sector pupils should, *ceteris paribus*, enrol on the UK's top courses. But they don't, partly because the schools don't encourage them to do so and partly because, reflecting the social culture around them, they don't feel the top universities are for them.

It will of course be argued that the private schools, buoyed up by rich endowments, tax subsidies from the Charity Commission, the best teachers trained at public expense and then bought up from the state sector, and much smaller class sizes, provide the education needed to incubate the nation's next leaders. But the harm done by private education is rarely weighed in the balance. Siphoning off bright middle-class children into private schools segregates talent instead of infusing it throughout the system and leaves the weaker elements of the state sector struggling and often sinking (the so-called 'failing schools'). But apart from skimming, British private schools create a detached elite with an often repressed emotional psychology. The psychotherapist Nick Duffell in a definitive study of the boarding school system[103] found that the boarding prep school, by separating children from their parents at the age of eight (or even younger), caused these artificial orphans to survive the loss of their families by dissociating themselves from their feelings of love, involving 'an extreme hardening of normal human softness, a severe cutting off from emotions and sensitivity'. This repressed emotion, with an encouragement instead to invest their natural loyalties in the institution, all too often rendered the adult product later a ready purveyor of hierarchy, suppression, dominance and class superiority.

Such a mindset and values are not conducive to the creation of an inclusive, balanced or compassionate society. Yet according to

---

103 Duffell, N., *The Making of Them: The British Attitude to Children and the Boarding School System*, Lone Arrow Press, 2000.

the Milburn report of 2009, some 75 per cent of judges, 70 per cent of finance directors, 45 per cent of top civil servants, 53 per cent of top journalists and 32 per cent of MPs come from this provenance. Even in John Major's 'classless' government, sixteen of the twenty male members of the 1993 cabinet had come from public schools, including twelve who had boarded.[104] This privately educated 7 per cent of the population not only dominates politics, the civil service and judiciary, but also the armed forces, the City, the media, the arts, academia, the most prestigious professions – and even the protest movements challenging these powers. An inbred sense of superiority and insensitivity towards the lower orders might make for highly effective colonial servants of empire, but whether such a distorted, even damaged, psychology would produce the teamwork, co-operativeness and shared inspiration needed by a modern complex, technological enterprise is quite another matter.

What is fundamentally at fault with the English educational system is its extreme selectivity, with the wealthiest segment creamed off into a segregated elite while the rest, hamstrung by a comparative paucity of resources and facilities, struggles hard to compete but can never equalise, leaving the tail-end to sink where the interconnected disadvantages of the underclass all come together. This long-existing pattern is now being accentuated by Gove's advocacy of 'free market' schools and academies. The former are modelled on the Swedish free schools project, yet academic research there has shown that it was expensive, it delivered only a very small increase in educational attainment, and at the same time it increased social inequality.[105] The latter,

---

104 Monbiot, G., *Guardian*, 22 January 2008.
105 *The Economist*, 20 May 2011.

academies, which when introduced in the 2000s had to be all-ability
and were focused on poorer areas (some with 50 per cent of pupils
eligible for free meals), have been transformed into instruments of
selection throughout the state sector, partly through taking very
few pupils on free school meals (1–2 per cent) and partly through
grammar schools being allowed to become academies.

(3) INTEGRATING THE PRIVATE SCHOOLS

If the goals are raising attainment, breaking down class segre-
gation and creating a more socially cohesive society with a
well-informed and activist citizenry, international studies show
clearly that countries that achieve both high standards and high
equity like Finland, Canada and South Korea have comprehensive systems. The alternatives, selective systems like Germany,
rank poorly both for achievement and equity in OECD's PISA
studies.[106] Finland, which tops the rankings, thrives with properly resourced comprehensives full of well-trained teachers and
without selective schools to compete against. Following the
precedent of these countries, the UK should abolish selection by
ability and outlaw other forms of social selection that continue
to discriminate against the poorest children. Local authorities shouldn't 'run' schools, which they haven't done for several
decades, but rather ensure fair funding, encourage collaboration,
and oversee special needs, admissions, exclusions and high-
quality early years provision. So-called independent state schools
should be brought back into the maintained system where the
rights of pupils, teachers and parents are properly protected.

But this process will not be complete unless the private schools

---

106 Millar, F., *Chartist*, July 2007.

are also integrated into the rest of society, both educationally and socially. Nor is this such a radical break as some might think. Contrary to the projected image of excellence, Ofsted in their 2008 report found that only 5 per cent of the 433 private schools reviewed rated 'outstanding' quality, some 6 per cent were 'inadequate', and the rest varied between 'satisfactory' and 'good' – a slightly worse overall record than the state schools, where 15 per cent were outstanding. The resistance will of course be centred on the top twenty or so of the Headmasters' Conference because that is where the privileges of the wealthiest class will be most challenged. Nevertheless the case against preserving an institution that seriously undermines all the rest of the educational sector and generates a repressed elite attuned to flaunt superiority over others is overwhelming.

There are various mechanisms by which this reform could be carried through. There is every justification to remove the tax subsidies private schools receive as 'charities' (some £100 million a year), but that would simply concentrate pupil entry even more exclusively on the richest families. Alternatively there is a good case for quotas: some 27,000 students achieve three A level A grades, a third from fee-charging schools and two-thirds from state schools. Requiring universities to reflect that balance would significantly improve the life chances of students from the poorer 90 per cent of the population, above all the 60,000 a year who score in the top 20 per cent in tests at eleven, fourteen and sixteen but still drop out of higher education. And there is further justification for such a move when research by the Sutton Trust in 2010 found that a comprehensive pupil with grades BBB was likely to perform as well in their university degree as a private or grammar school pupil with two As and a B. Or, thirdly, the proposals of the Donnison Commission on the Public Schools could be revisited, requiring at set intervals first 25 per cent, then 50 per cent, then 75 per cent and finally all the intake into the private schools to be chosen at random from the wider population. Indeed these three alternatives are not mutually exclusive. There are certainly good grounds for ending tax subsidies straight away, then quotas for university entrance could be quickly introduced, followed by the Donnison Commission proposals for the steady rise in random recruitment to the private schools until full integration was achieved.

CHAPTER XV

REINFORCING THE PUBLIC SERVICE ETHOS

Another central purpose of national interest capitalism is to reinvigorate those areas of public life which have fallen into serious decay and are now badly failing the nation. In accordance with that criterion this chapter examines each main area of social policy, with particular reference to the role which only a resuscitated state can play in securing a revival. That entails a very different role for the state – not privatised (as Blair wanted), not centralised (as Brown wanted), not eviscerated (as Cameron wants) – but rather an open, activist, empowering, participatory function that meets needs where the market fails.

(I) MEETING THE HUGE GAP IN HOUSING NEED

Perhaps the biggest failure in meeting fundamental household needs and the biggest repository of social misery in Britain today lies in the collapse of social housing provision. Apart from the three-quarters of the population who own their own homes, the remaining quarter, who are overwhelmingly the poorest, are housed by private landlords, housing associations or local authorities. Thatcher's drive to privatise the housing sector through the 1985 right to buy at heavily discounted prices, followed by New Labour's enforced sell-off of much of the rest, decimated social housing. The number of houses built by local authorities dwindled rapidly under Thatcher from over 100,000 a year in 1979 to less than 16,380 in 1990, then to just 450 under Major in 1996–7, and finally under Blair–Brown to an average of only 160 a year, equivalent to building one house a year per four constituencies. This is despite a recent estimate that while an average of around 162,000 houses have been completed annually over the last ten years, an additional 232,000 households are expected to be formed each year over the next twenty years or so,[107] a large proportion within the poorer income brackets.

Yet the Tory–Lib Dem coalition is now cutting the already hugely depleted social housing budget by 60 per cent, with the ensuing collapse in the building of affordable housing to be recouped by allowing rents to be charged on future new-build housing at 80 per cent of the private market rate. This would more than double existing rent levels which, in conjunction with £18 billion welfare payment cuts and big housing benefit cuts and an overall benefit cap being imposed at the same time, must inevitably push the lowest-income 15–20 per cent of the population (9–12 million people) into housing poverty, if not homelessness.

There are already 100,000 people who are homeless, and a further 1.8 million households on waiting lists seeking a house or flat from the local council. The private house-building industry is at a nadir, with lower completions in 2010 than in any year since 1923. Only the state has the capacity to redress this unconscionable housing squeeze for the lowest-paid quarter of the population. What is needed is the abandonment of the ideological dogma that all housing must be privatised, which this quartile can never afford, and the adoption of a new target to build high-quality public housing on a sufficient scale to clear the council and housing association waiting lists within ten to fifteen years and to replace all unfit, damp and decaying housing. Only the state has the capability to drive this massive new public sector programme of building affordable housing for rent, which would also offer the additional benefits of increasing employment, raising tax revenues and galvanising a moribund private house-building industry. It initially should be funded, as indicated in Chapter XIII (5–6), by a wealth tax or an annual capital gains tax, which would largely transfer property from the richest part of the population to the poorest sections, and would gradually become self-funding as a result of reduced unemployment and steadily rising tax receipts.

(2) REDRESSING THE HUGE FAILURE OF PRIVATISED PENSIONS

During the neo-liberal ascendancy of the last thirty years both Tory and New Labour governments changed the balance of pension provision from predominantly public to predominantly private. Barbara Castle's 1968 State Earnings-Related Pension Scheme (SERPS), which significantly raised pension levels, particularly for the low-paid and for women, but which also permitted contracting out provided the standards of the scheme's guaranteed minimum pension were met, was first gutted by Fowler in 1986 and then finally replaced altogether by the Blair government. This was done to pave the way for privatised pensions, yet experience has shown that these are entirely at the mercy of employer arrangements and stock market returns. As a result, nearly half of those in the private sector, between ten million and fifteen million workers, have no occupational pension at all. Final salary schemes, where they do still exist in the private sector, are being rapidly wound up. And pension payouts to private sector workers have fallen by as much as two-thirds, partly because of a falling stock market but also because employer contributions have halved in recent years – notably through employers unilaterally taking 'pension holidays' and not paying into their schemes while still requiring their employees to do so.

The private market cannot guarantee pension rights because of the continuous economic cycles within capitalism. Collective national provision of pensions is superior for three key reasons. One is that all insurance schemes (i.e. saving against future risk) are more secure the larger the insurance (in this case the pension) pot because it evens out the cyclical upturns and downturns and counteracts breakdowns in employment experience. Secondly the state, uniquely, has the ultimate power to underwrite the pension, which is, after all, deferred pay. And thirdly, there are too many examples of abuse of pension funds (from Robert Maxwell's stealing pension money to stave off his own bankruptcy to semi-privatised Royal Mail last year risking £5 billion of pension scheme cash on equity futures bets) to trust the private sector with guardianship of all the nation's pensions.

At present several million employees in both the private and public sectors contribute all their working lives and still end up with a pension below the means-tested pension credit line, which means they contributed for nothing since they would still anyway have received income support. What therefore is needed is a new high-value, high-quality state secondary pension scheme – on top of the now miserably shrunken low-level basic state pension – which is earnings related rather than flat rate and which guarantees pension levels for all well above the poverty line. It would be phased in gradually but steadily over a ten-to-fifteen-year period, as spelt out in Chapter XIII (4).

(3) RESTORING THE VALUES OF ALTRUISM AND PUBLIC SERVICE IN HEALTH

The gradual marketisation of health services during the neo-liberal period formed the most serious inroad into the principles and goals of public services over the last thirty years. Thatcher introduced the internal market into the NHS, and New Labour took the process further by converting NHS trusts into independent businesses (foundation trusts), setting up private treatment centres (ISTCs) paid for by public funds irrespective of the number of patients treated, giving NHS work to private hospitals and clinics and encouraging NHS patients to choose them, and developing commissioning on a health maintenance organisation (HMO) basis as in the US.

The Tory–Lib Dem coalition in 2011 then took this much further. The requirement on the proposed new GPs' consortia to commission services from 'any qualified provider' as opposed to, previously, the NHS as 'the preferred provider' paved the way for the full-scale privatisation of the NHS. Moreover it opened up the NHS for the first time to EU competition law. That means GP consortia, if they are to avoid legal action by private companies, must put all contracts out to tender. And to whittle down the role of public service further, the new NHS operating framework allows providers to offer services 'at less than the published manda-tory tariff price', thus giving the private sector the opening to offer temporary loss leaders which undercut the NHS. This represents the end of the NHS as a universal and accountable public service.

The inherent drawbacks of private markets in health are clear.

Price competition, explicitly introduced by Lansley's Bill at paragraph 5.43 of his NHS Operating Framework, will undermine quality standards. A health market will fragment the NHS by squeezing out long-trusted local hospitals through private competitors creaming off the most lucrative parts of the service. The integrity of GPs will be compromised by putting them in charge of commercial decisions over commissioning from which they themselves could profit. The likelihood that GP consortia will contract with private companies (e.g. Bupa, Capita, Serco, Virgin, or US multinational healthcare corporations like Humana, United Healthcare or McKinsey) to advise them on their contracting role will create a serious conflict of interest when the same private companies become both purchaser and provider. The government's lifting the cap on hospitals' private earnings means NHS patients could well find themselves pushed to the back of the queue. The weight of evidence is also that private markets in health bring exorbitant administrative costs, which are likely in the UK to triple from 6 per cent now to probably 20 per cent by 2014. This will lead to cherry-picking of more profitable patients, increase inequity and the postcode lottery gap, and intensify pressure for top-up payments and 'care package' limits.

The case for reversing these measures is overwhelming. The popular demand, supported by the Royal Colleges, for the highest possible quality of care free at the point of service, equity between all patients based exclusively on need, universality without fragmentation of the service, and accountability through democratic channels, can only be met by a public service supervised by the state and headed by a Cabinet Secretary of State for Health. That doesn't mean that the NHS shouldn't be

REINFORCING THE PUBLIC SERVICE ETHOS 227

subject to regular examination (as opposed to successive top-down wholesale reorganisations) to ensure value for money, squeeze out waste and keep bureaucracy to a minimum, incentivise the morale and highest performance of staff at all levels, and rebalance the service increasingly towards community and preventive care. But it does mean that the principles of a universal public service must be sacrosanct, and that is incompatible with private markets.

(4) EMBEDDING INCLUSIVENESS AND EQUALITY IN EDUCATION

Ever since comprehensive education was introduced in 1965, there have been persistent attempts to reintroduce selection by the back door, ostensibly to promote excellence among the brightest pupils, in reality to give preferential advantage to the middle classes anxious to circumvent a level playing field of meritocracy fair for all. Private schools and a core of grammar schools were retained which preserved selection, the assisted places scheme and city technology colleges were started under Thatcher–Major to cream off a select group of pupils, academies were begun under Blair to semi-privatise a growing segment of secondary education, and both academies and so-called 'free schools' are being further disseminated across the spectrum by Cameron–Gove. All these measures undercut fair educational opportunity for all.

Banding arrangements may allow academies to introduce selection covertly, while private sponsors raise serious questions about accountability and due governance. By announcing that all schools judged 'outstanding' by Ofsted will be pre-approved for academy status, Gove is conferring extra benefits on some of the most socially exclusive schools in the country. Analysis of schools judged 'outstanding' by Ofsted has found that they take 40 per cent fewer poor pupils than the national average, while some schools in the most deprived communities have as many as half their pupils eligible for free school meals. This outcome will be reinforced when academies, which previously had to be all-ability, can take in grammar schools, which often have levels of free school meals pupils of only 1–2 per cent.

This process of increasing social exclusivity in education is being taken further by two other policy developments. One is Gove's introduction of 'free schools' on the Swedish model, which has been hailed as the opportunity for parents to break free and create their own excellence in their neighbourhood. However, what has driven this development in Sweden is not the search for higher standards for all (they were already very high), but rather antagonism to the growing number of immigrant children and the wish to keep 'Swedish' pupils separate. Even if this proposal were to be taken up in significant numbers in the UK, it is likely that the great majority of parents attracted to this idea will have neither the time, the skills nor the inclination to do the job themselves and will recruit private sector partners to do it for them. Thus the outcome will be growing privatisation of the UK education system and an extended reintroduction of selection.

The other area where exclusivity is being enhanced further is in access to higher education. Last year only 2.6 per cent of the 2,800 intake to Oxford came from disadvantaged areas, 3.5 per cent in the case of Cambridge, and 5 per cent in the case of Bristol, LSE, UCL, King's College London, and Imperial College. Whereas fifteen years ago bright children from the richest homes were six times more likely than equally bright children from the poorest homes to get a place in the top third of universities, now they are seven times more likely to do so. This differential is set to widen as the £30 a week educational maintenance allowance, designed to enable pupils to stay on at school to gain access to tertiary education, is abolished, while the tripling of tuition fees at universities to nearly £9,000 a year is bound to discourage applications from pupils from poorer homes.[108] Again a US-style higher education market is being opened up to allow the rich and privileged to gain greater exclusivity.

By contrast, the only means by which all pupils, irrespective of class and income, can gain equal opportunity to realise their full potential is through state provision at the highest quality level of the whole range of education – in effect, a world-class national education service to match the world-class NHS. This is the pattern already followed by the countries with the best educational record, notably Finland and (until recently) Sweden. It is strongly justified by the fact that the pool of talent is inevitably limited, and in a highly competitive educational and economic environment a significant sacrifice of it for any reason cannot be permitted. Clearly there has been a huge waste of talent in the UK over several decades for a variety of reasons – class, income, culture, differential parental aspiration, economic pressures – and since Britain's long-term decline is closely related to its class-ridden and underperforming educational system, redressing that imbalance is a prime requirement for Britain's recovery.

Specifically it requires several profound reforms. The private schools and remaining grammar schools need to be brought

---

108 UK applicants to UK universities were down by 8.9 per cent in 2012 compared with the previous year, according to UCAS applicant statistics 21 September 2012 and UCAS online data tables. The fall is likely to be considerably larger in 2012/13, when average tuition fees will more than double.

into the wider national system of education, whether by gradual absorption, as recommended by the Donnison Committee of 1967, removal of charitable status, financial incentives as an escape route from a growing costs squeeze or, ultimately, if necessary by public takeover. Significantly higher performance outcomes should be set to achieve at least the much higher academic and technological standards already demonstrated by immediate competitors like France and Germany, and an English baccalaureate with high pass rates should be established as the key target for all secondary schools. In the poorest parts of the country catering for an underclass numbering perhaps 10–15 per cent of the population, strong incentives should be offered to best-quality teachers to take up the challenge to transform such schools, and a much bigger and sustained campaign should be launched, going out into the catchment community to try to secure parents' commitment to the long-term rewards of (much) improved educational performance by their children.

Universalising the benefits of higher education can be funded from a range of sources. Governments should make at least some contribution to ensure that bright pupils from poorer households are not locked out of equal opportunity by excessive upfront costs. Universities, particularly the older ones which have inherited enormous endowment income over the centuries, should also contribute according to their means, or perhaps via a carousel system or perhaps by some agreed sharing of costs between them. Business, which will derive its future leading personnel from universities, should be expected to pay a proportion of the costs for the recruitment of its future profit-drivers, just as it should also pay for the skill training of its manual employees. Parents of university students, overwhelmingly middle class and disproportionately upper middle class, should also make some contribution, on a tapered scale above a certain income level up to full payment at high levels. And the students themselves should also be expected to pay back some modest proportion of the extra increment of earning power that university education has accorded them.

(5) ESTABLISHING ADULT SOCIAL CARE AS A FREE UNIVERSAL SERVICE

The Cameron policy of opening up all state provision to 'any qualified provider' represents the logical extreme of privatisation of public services. The consequences of the policy in terms of the stability and continuity of services have recently become most pressing in the field of social care, but also apply to every other service category in private hands. What happens if the private provider goes bankrupt, is bought out by other corporate interests that do not wish to continue the service, or is closed down by the regulator (the Care Quality Commission) for gross failure in standards? Once large-scale public provision has been dispensed with, there may be few or no options for continuing the service for its current recipients.

This problem has recently become most acute over residential provision for elderly people. The Tory government policy in the 1990s of incentivising the switch to private providers led over the following two decades to the opening of private and voluntary homes with 110,000 beds at the same time as 95,000 closed in local authority homes. Today some 90 per cent of residential care provision is not publicly provided and most is for profit, yet no plans were ever made or perhaps even ever contemplated for when a major provider collapsed or downsized. At the same time, driven by very tight financial controls from Whitehall, councils offered such minimal rates to pay for elderly people in care (some paying only £400 a week when even minimum care cannot be provided for less than £480 a week) that small private providers were squeezed out of business. Then with a Whitehall preference for large-scale providers – ironically, to ensure the security of long-term care – homes for elderly people began to be floated on the market in exactly the same way as metal or food commodities, according to which purchases could be made the most profitable. In the most high-profile recent case Southern Cross, the largest private care-home chain in the UK with 750 care homes housing 31,000 elderly people (mostly in their eighties and nineties and many with dementia), was threatened with collapse because its private equity owners creamed off the lucrative freeholds and left the company insolvent by being unable to lease back the properties.

With private capital scouring the world for the best returns but with no moral sense of quality of performance, reliability or long-term commitment (Blackstone, the world's largest private equity operator, being recently reported to be 'running a slide rule over nursing homes'), such problems of rapid, unceremonious disposal are bound to recur in other fields, including health, education, housing, pensions, childcare and prison management, among others. And while they are subject to regulation of minimum standards, they are not driven by the ethics of equity, accountability and optimum outcomes for the recipient, which direct the provision of public services.

The funding liabilities of the present privatised system of adult social care are simply unmanageable. In 2012 the Local Government Association announced that the gap between the money available that year and the predicted cost of these services was £1.4 billion, stretching to £16.5 billion by 2020 when it was predicted that spending on social care would exceed 45 per cent of council budgets. Yet this dilemma is not insoluble. The long-term cost of the Dilnot Commission proposals for social care is estimated at £3 billion a year – as it happens, the same sum as Osborne chose to give away instead in his 2012 Budget to the 1 per cent earning over £3,000 a week by his cut in the 50p rate of tax. In the longer term, however, as care costs steadily rise and the numbers of over-65s are predicted by Osborne's Office of Budget Responsibility to rise from 17 per cent now to 26 per cent over the next fifty years, the only way to contain the costs while also guaranteeing high-quality standards of care is by a new social insurance scheme. Clearly it could only be introduced gradually over a decade or so, and in the meantime the Dilnot recommendations offer a reasonable compromise between acceptable costs and proper standards.

(6) THE NEED FOR A NEW PUBLIC SERVICE IN LEGAL RIGHTS

The principle of free access to justice, established as part of the post-1945 settlement, was seen as no less fundamental a right than education or healthcare. In 2006, after the cost of legal aid had risen in the previous decade to £2 billion a year, the Carter review was set up to introduce market principles and sharply reduce costs. At root, Carter's proposal was to stop paying lawyers by the hour and instead pay them a fixed price for each job done. But because most legal aid operators are not big firms but small high street practices whose income was reduced by some 40 per cent by Carter's strictures, a large number went bust. While previously many were motivated to work in this less lucra-tive branch of the law by social conscience, now the model was small firms merging and making 'efficiencies' in their IT costs and back-office work, then surviving firms having to compete in price-competitive tendering, and finally jostling to come in below the fixed rate so that only the leanest and meanest would survive. What this has meant is the remaining firms running a glorified call centre, with a floor of staff untrained in the law patrolled by a roaming solicitor checking quality. Poor clients become represented by paralegals and novice lawyers, facing prosecution teams often armed with ever greater resources.

Growing inequality before the law has become compounded by the loss of other implicit services. Many lawyers previously operated as unofficial social workers, but that has been largely swept away, and when legal aid is now less available to solve the myriad civil disputes that arise every day, the immediate bill has gone down, leaving a larger one to pay in social costs down the line. Many defence lawyers, too, have crossed sides to take advantage of the better pensions and longer holidays available to staff in the Crown Prosecution Service. Defence work in big cities is therefore increasingly undertaken by a handful of mega-firms dependent on the government for contracts and therefore with little of the independence expected of the legal profession in a democracy.

What is really needed is far more profound reform of the legal process than the narrow remit of the Carter review. The review ignored the real reasons behind the rise in legal aid bills. It is partly because there has previously been suppressed demand for access to justice, but also because new technology, from DNA testing to CCTV, plus a barrage of new laws, involves more extensive and more complex work. Neither is a good reason for undermining the key principle of equality before the law, on which every democracy depends, and neither warrants the introduction of market mechanisms which load the balance in favour of cheapness over justice. In addition the market model has both intensified the increasingly aggressive confrontation between barristers and solicitors as well as pressurising a win at all costs rather than mediating solutions to the best satisfaction of both parties.

But most fundamentally of all, what is needed is the introduction of a public salaried legal service covering all welfare issues, including landlord and tenant issues, matrimonial and childcare disputes, immigration matters, employment rights, health and safety, benefit entitlements and indebtedness problems. While commercial law and corporate disputes would be lucrative areas left to private lawyers, those fields of personal welfare on which equal rights and opportunities basically depend would be free at the point of need for all citizens, largely paid for, like health and education, out of taxation and filtered by a much revamped Legal Services Commission. In the situation of austerity of the early 2010s, the funding of this crucial service can readily come largely from the richest section of the population who in both income and wealth terms have over the last three decades been so grossly under-taxed or have avoided tax altogether through extensive use of tax havens.

CHAPTER XVI

THE QUEST FOR DEMOCRATIC ACCOUNTABILITY

(I) THE CONTINUING ASCENDANCY OF CORPORATE POWER

Despite the colossal setback of the Great Crash of 2008–9, the power structure of neo-liberal capitalism has remained remarkably intact, partly because of the force of its previous hegemony, but also because of the current state of political culture and ideology (or lack of it) as well as the disarray of potential counter-forces. Neo-liberalism is not so much an economic ideology as a power system. Thus in the US Reagan harnessed the power of the state to crush labour unions as a political entity, to undermine the lawyers defending liberal causes, and to attack the left's base through the privatisation of social security. In the UK, Thatcher mobilised state power, most notably against the miners to crush the trade union movement by eviscerating its strongest component, but also by a systematic programme of privatisation of industry and by inroads into public services aimed at marketising them. Her greatest triumph was to mobilise a political coalition of the more prosperous elements in the working class together with most of the middle and upper classes and use it to overturn the post-war settlement, the immediate purpose being political – to implant permanently the anti-state ideology – but as she herself candidly admitted: 'Economics are the method; the object is to change the soul.'

Globally since 1979 the new world order has been orchestrated and overseen by a worldwide cosmopolitan super-class combining the financial and political elites. It brings together the chief executives of top multinational corporations, hedge fund managers, investment bankers and pension fund managers on the one hand and central bankers, finance ministers and other key political leaders on the other. It represents, loosely but effectively organised, the multi-trillion-pound privatisation of the global economy's funding, largely above and beyond political control. It worked in co-operation with, and was backed by, the multilateral institutions created at Bretton Woods in 1944 – the IMF, World Bank and GATT (transformed in 1995 into the World Trade Organization) – intergovernmental bodies dominated by the most powerful country, the US, and reflecting the values and interests of the global governing elite. Hence despite the unprecedented magnitude of the worldwide financial and economic crisis since 2008, this elite has been determined at any cost to return to business as usual in order to preserve its controlling dominance over the international economy.

The British elite, once portrayed as forming a series of interconnected and overlapping circles of influence[109] with ties of family, class, education and genteel manners, was transformed under the influence of neo-liberalism into a much more hard-nosed and mercenary force focused more ruthlessly around the goals of wealth and market power. These operators of the big corporations

---

109   Sampson, A., *Anatomy of Britain*, Hodder & Stoughton, 1962.

usurped much of the power previously vested in government and used it to divert public life to their own private ends.

Examples abound across the spectrum. The provision of hospitals, schools, roads and prisons has been tailored to meet corporate requirements rather than public need. In most industrial sectors half a dozen major companies have emerged as oligopolies with substantial lobbying muscle in Whitehall but relatively impervious to public influence. Superstores notably have gained their pre-eminence by strangling smaller shops and squeezing their suppliers. Urban regeneration programmes have been subverted to favour the interests of private companies, while the granting of planning permission, once the rigorous exercise of public rectitude, may now be simply offered for sale to the highest bidder. Biotech companies have tried to turn the food chain into a manipulated commodity, aided by a network of government relationships to gain favourable regulation. The corporate takeover of schools and universities has gathered pace, distorting research and teaching agendas to serve business interests more closely. Health and safety protections, environmental standards and labour regulations are subject to constant pressure to whittle them down in order to free up business at the expense of the public interest.

The relentless spread of privatisation over the last thirty years has meant that corporate power now reaches into every niche of government, finance, media, law and international relations. The corporate takeover of Britain has reached the point where it can be argued that it now holds liberal democracy in thrall.[110] It is that nexus of corporate power with the organs of the state at

---

110   Monbiot, G., *The Captive State*, Macmillan, 2000.

every level – international, national, regional and local – which has made the power structure of the market state so difficult to dislodge, exactly as Thatcher intended.

That corporate dominance is mirrored by the weakness of the Labour Party and its trade union allies (membership down from 12 million in 1980 to 6.5 million today). A severe economic crisis such as the crash of 2008–9 does not by itself generate change in the absence of a mass movement demanding a radical alternative. Historically, social democracy emerged at least partly as a social and political concession to prevent more radical social change (as the Tory Lord Hailsham noted in 1943, 'if you don't give people social reform, they are going to give you social revolution'). Those necessary forces in the second decade of the twenty-first century remain attenuated by Thatcher's series of six anti-trade union laws (1980–90), Blair's systematic squeezing out of the political left in manipulated parliamentary selections, and above all the Blair–Brown wholesale adoption of the Thatcherite neo-liberal ideology, effectively making Britain a one-party state fed by two parties with a largely overlapping agenda.

This corporate dominance was further reinforced by the collapse of any significant counter-ideology. The idea was sedulously peddled in the 1980–90s by the neo-liberal advocates that the debt-fuelled market that had existed in the US and UK for little more than a decade was the only economic system consistent with the imperatives of modernity and was destined to spread universally. Globalisation was then perceived as no more than the Anglo-American free market writ large, and its triumph over any dissent for two decades was so comprehensive that when it abruptly imploded in 2008 even the instruments of state intervention were made subservient to neo-liberal goals.

Thus nationalisation in 2008–9 gave control of the banks RBS and Lloyds to the state, but instead of being used to enforce increased lending to small businesses and to restrain top pay and bonus excesses, they were allowed to continue at arm's length on a business-as-usual scenario without any quid pro quo. All political parties throughout the West have become so saturated by the neo-liberal mindset that even in its eclipse they lack the confidence to break with its shibboleths. And the great majority of the think tanks, reinforced by largesse on the right, continue unabated to put out a consistent agenda – to oppose the laws which protect the public from banks and corporations, to demand the privatisation of state assets, to argue that the rich should pay less tax, and to pour scorn on global warming.

(2) WHY HAVE THE CHECKS ON CORPORATE POWER BEEN SO INEFFECTIVE?

The three organs in society for securing accountability against excessive or abusive power are the media, whose prime role should be to hold power to account, the politicians, who should be arbiters holding the ring against conflicting or destructive interests, and the police, who should be enforcing the law without fear or favour to external parties. All three have failed in their prime duty or have succumbed to pressure or ingratiation from corporate power.

(i) The media

If the UK media is to be an effective constraint on corporate excess, as opposed to an accomplice in it, far-reaching changes are needed in its structure, ownership, orientation and mode of operation. Press ownership should be limited to UK citizens and subject to a fit-for-purpose test, both of which counts would likely exclude Murdoch. News Corporation at its height controlled 37 per cent of the UK newspaper market, far too great a concentration of power in such a sensitive area as agenda-setting in a democracy – even without that power being used, as has now been revealed, to intimidate individuals and to pressurise governments to conform to his will. Clearly, in terms of both fostering diversity and preventing use of excessive power there should be a mandatory restriction on any one person or organisation controlling more than one daily and one Sunday paper. Similarly, the law restricting monopolistic cross-media ownership between broadcast and print media, which Thatcher swept to one side in the early 1980s and thus set Murdoch on his way to real power, should be reinstated and strengthened.

Other structural reforms are needed if the media is to perform its proper function in society. A right of reply needs to be instituted in the UK, along lines established in many other countries, and the feeble and toothless Press Complaints Commission, dominated by newspaper editors rather than independently regulating them, should be replaced. One alternative option is the co-regulation model currently operated in Denmark, where a broadly self-regulating media is balanced by a regulatory council that can go to law when it needs to enforce its judgements. But what is needed from the Leveson inquiry is a wholly new framework for media accountability – one that will guarantee genuine independence for editors, a conscience clause for journalists' right to act according to some agreed code of practice and ethics, but also protection for the public from rogue journalists who could face de-registration if they persistently use prohibited practices to gather material.

Equally crucially, there is an acute need for greater diversity in the media when overwhelmingly it is concentrated around a broad (pro-corporate) cultural consensus to the exclusion of a wide range of minority views. At present the only constraint is the arcane 'plurality' provision in the 2003 Communications Act, which allows the UK Business Secretary to refer any bid involving cross-media ownership to Ofcom to ensure it will not materially reduce the plurality of voice in the British media. But this is a wholly inadequate and uncertain mechanism to ensure diversity, especially since Ofcom's view has to be forwarded to the Competition Commission for the final decision. The market, however, will not produce the pluralism that democracy needs. Journalism in the public interest or as a public good is less profitable – celebrity gossip makes money, much less investigations into the financial sector – so it will require new forms of funding such as advertising levies or state-assisted start-up funding according to agreed predetermined criteria. Scandinavia and the Netherlands use forms of public support for secondary local newspapers to ensure plurality.

One other important remaining question is: how can balance and impartiality be better obtained when at present press ownership is largely in the hands of wealthy tycoons who orientate their titles to their own values and world view and thus as a group regularly portray a very one-sided take on events and their meaning? Impartiality matters when people want objectivity, not propaganda (a major reason why the BBC is so popular), and when bias can gravely distort not only the daily national agenda but the political culture of a generation. An effective regulatory body should use its rulings to buttress objectivity and honest statement of the facts, while diminishing the opportunity subliminally to present a coloured and selective version designed to prejudice readers' opinions in a particular direction. Another requirement, particularly in the context of declining newspaper finances, would be the supplementing of revenues by a public fund, administered strictly at arm's length from government, designed broadly to equalise funding between groups of newspapers according to the proportion of votes received by the party they supported at the last election. But at present, in the absence of all these reforms, the broad conclusion must be that the press, so far from independently holding corporate power to account (with honourable exceptions such as *The Guardian*), is actually in practice one of the main channels for the exercise of that power.

(ii) The police

While local policing is highly popular with the public and moderately effective, the exercise of the policing function at the highest level is quite another matter. The relationship between the police on the one hand and political governance and corporate dominance on the other is necessarily an uneasy one, treading a difficult line between independent enforcement and falling prey to pressure from, or manipulation by, political leaders or corporate power-brokers. Thatcher's mobilisation of the police as a paramilitary force against the miners in 1985 was an example of the former, while the phone-hacking scandal uncovered in 2011 revealed the latter.

Britain is so regulation-lite that the insidious and sinister power structure between the police, No. 10 and the media remained concealed for decades. The only other country that has permitted such self-reinforcing networks of business, political and enforcement power is Italy, with the baleful results displayed in the Berlusconi era. The hacking revelations of 2011–12 showed that a quarter of Scotland Yard press officers had worked at News International, that the *News of the World*'s chief reporter, Neville Thurlbeck, was an official police informer, that the hiring by Scotland Yard of Neil Wallis, the former deputy editor of the *News of the World*, was so casual, with no due diligence at all, as to suggest the Met and News International were symbiotically linked, and that Wallis continued to act as an informal adviser to Andy Coulson even when the latter was ensconced at No. 10. The classic Home Office response – to set up a new code of police–media ethics – is clearly inadequate in the light of exposure of profound dereliction of duty by police at the highest level and the taking of bribes estimated at £130,000 for illegally passing on private information.

Nor are the phone-hacking revelations a unique example of high-level police collusion. The likely police connivance in the construction industry blacklisting operation over forty years, which denied employment to some 3,400 building workers because they were trade unionists or health and safety representatives on building sites that are death traps and regularly lead to forty to fifty deaths a year, is another example. One of the victims of this blacklisting has argued in court that some of the information 'could only have been supplied by the police or the security service', while a former police officer has publicly stated that data from the seized records 'reads like police reconnaissance reports'.[111] A further example is the extreme tactics adopted by police handlers against environmental protestors, even to the extent of undercover officers forming long-term liaisons with targeted suspects, all at the behest of big energy

---

111   *Observer*, 29 July 2012.

companies eager to squeeze out any public dissent from their corporate plans and having the police in tow for activities out of all proportion to what can be morally or financially justified.

Dealing with such collusion and even deep-seated and pervasive corruption as has been exposed requires much more stringent and pro-active strategic supervision. This will not be provided by the Independent Police Complaints Commission, which is a body for investigating individual complaints not for pursuing criminality in high places where the damage is really done. Nor will it come from Ofcom, which does not have this remit either, and anyway has inadequate powers. What is needed is a new body with much greater powers to check abuse and investigate evidence which may point to corruption, similar to the role of the Securities and Exchange Commission in the financial arena. Yet it is precisely the very close power nexus between the police/security services and Downing Street which will use every means available to block any such reform. Again, it is clear from this analysis that at the highest level of the power structure the police are more likely to be complicit with corporate interests rather than a stringent regulator of them.

(iii) Political governance

The governance framework at the political level is defined by the constant struggle between three conflicting tensions – the continuing attempts by government to extend its reach and enhance its powers, the efforts of the elected parliament to constrain the excesses of government and hold it to account, and the endless devices of vested interests and a wide array of private, voluntary and charitable concerns to obtain legislative support, funding or general government backing to secure their objectives. At the present time the currents are still running strongly in favour of an ever more powerful executive and ever more insidious and corrupting penetration of the governing system by outside corporate lobbying interests, while efforts to restore accountability by Parliament are merely incipient and fragmentary.

The tightening politico-corporate nexus, particularly over the last three decades, is partly shown by the more skilful and professional corporate lobbying deployed, the growth of in-house government relations units in large companies, and the secrecy with which they can operate uninhibited by any public regulations.[112] But it is even more clearly revealed by the increasingly incestuous revolving door between ministers and the private sector, with ministers often leaving Whitehall to become directors or consultants at companies which were linked to their departmental responsibilities. Correspondingly, outside appointments from the corporate sector increasingly abound in government departments, either as ministers, senior civil servants or members of task forces or advisory committees. A study found that in 2008 no fewer than twenty-eight former ministers had taken up jobs in the private sector over the previous two years while in many cases remaining as MPs, and by 2011 no fewer than thirty-one ex-ministers had done so over the previous year.[113] Barclays alone had fourteen revolving-door exchanges in both directions in 2009, while a further ten banks had more than five each.[114] The extent of 'revolving in' is shown by the fact that of those appointed to permanent secretary or director general posts, more than half were externally recruited, mostly from

---

112   House of Commons Public Administration Select Committee report, 2008.
113   Advisory Committee on Business Appointments, 2008 and 2011.
114   Miller, D., report for OECD, Strathclyde, 2009.

the private sector.[115] In addition, the coalition government after 2010 has upgraded departmental boards, half recruited from the private sector on a part-time basis, to the role of strategic and operational leadership in every government department.

This seamless interchange between ministers and the private sector has paved the way for the corporate takeover of government at the expense of democracy. Placing businessmen at the heart of government has clearly promoted further outsourcing and private sector involvement in every aspect of policy delivery, but it has also given them privileged contacts for future promotion of their own business interests. The ultimate sell-out to industry is revealed by Lansley's appointment of industry insiders to his 'responsibility deal' groups set up to tackle obesity and alcoholism, including representatives from McDonald's, KFC, Mars, and PepsiCo, with the alcohol group chaired by the chief executive of the Wine and Spirit Trade Association.[116] Under these influences the public sector's values and ethos have increasingly been transmuted to fit the private market's logic and interests, allowing the latter to permeate ever more deeply into the governing sphere.

In the face of this huge expansion of influence of professional corporate lobbyists, there is already some move within Parliament to lay down a mandatory public register which should include in each case the scope of their activities, the source of their funding and details of all their meetings with ministers, with deterrent sanctions against those who evade this essential transparency. Predictably, however, government is trying to neutralise its influence by making the register voluntary and denying effective

115   House of Commons Public Administration Select Committee, 2010.
116   Beetham, D., *Red Pepper*, October 2011.

sanctions. But the central point is that once again the politicians, like the police and the press, are no match for resisting the octopoid entanglements of corporate influence – indeed, they prefer a cosy relationship with corporate power that offers both potential personal rewards and an easier life.

The conclusions from this chapter are disturbing. Corporate power, despite the catastrophic financial and economic collapse extending from 2008–9, remains dominant, indeed hardly challenged. The institutions which should be keeping it in check have largely struck a Mephistophelean deal with it which, though shaken, remains intact. There is no early sign that this will change, though the perfect storm that is developing, involving global downturn, deepening eurozone crisis, economic contraction in many developed countries and growing public resistance to tightening budgets amid unprecedented austerity, may yet trigger an explosion which could enforce an abrupt transition to a very different business model.

PART 5

THE WIDER PERSPECTIVE

CHAPTER XVII

THE GLOBAL ARCHITECTURE OF NATIONAL INTEREST CAPITALISM

(I) THE NEED FOR A NEW WORLD ORDER

Parts 3 and 4 of this book have indicated that a system of capitalism which benefits the national interest of the population as a whole, as compared to a tiny economic–financial elite, requires very different economic and social underpinnings from the neo-liberal capitalism that prevailed over the near three decades of 1980–2008. Equally, it requires a different international governance model if it is to deal with the greatest challenges now facing the world's future – climate change, the scramble for gradually diminishing oil and energy supplies, over-exploitation of planetary natural resources, to mention just some – and indeed the global unfettered market system actually exacerbated these problems.

It is clear that the new multipolarity embracing China, the US, Europe, Japan, India and Russia, which contains 54 per cent of the world's population and 70 per cent of its GDP, no longer accepts international rules that once favoured a rich and powerful West. The IMF, once the monitor of exchange rates and lender of last resort to stricken governments, now finds many emerging economies awash with funds from waves of foreign direct investment, and is losing relevance especially as the Washington consensus weakens. Some argue instead for a World Investment

Organisation to set basic rules for the huge and complex cash flows now dominating world finance in hedge funds, sovereign wealth funds, banks and financial markets.

Moreover, contrary to the prevailing wisdom of the dominant elite in the US–UK (at least until 2008) that neo-liberalism offers the best route to world development, the evidence has now proved strongly to the contrary. Since 1980, when an integrated world economy really got under way, world GDP has grown only slightly more than half as fast as it did in the period before 1980. And in some respects its impacts have been quite malign. Joseph Stiglitz, as chief economist at the World Bank, identified the uncontrolled flow of 'hot money' as the main culprit of the east Asian tiger economy crisis of 1997–8, as well as behind the recurrent crises over the last decade in Mexico, Argentina, South Korea, Indonesia and Brazil, since footloose capital so often exacerbates the underlying cycles and generates instability.

For the poorer developing countries the impact has been stark. The share of global income of the poorest fifth of the world has actually halved since 1960 to a paltry 1.1 per cent today. World inequality has grown drastically. The twenty richest countries now have 125 times higher GDP per head than the twenty poorest countries. Not only has the spread of neo-liberalism across the world over the last three decades, even before 2007, increased the numbers forced to subsist on $2 a day to three billion people, they have also left forty-six countries actually poorer now than a decade ago.

Neo-liberalised trade policies have now resulted in fifty million more Africans in poverty than in 1997, and have brought huge job losses in Ghana, Kenya, Côte d'Ivoire, Morocco, Zimbabwe, Malawi (where real wages in manufacturing plunged 73 per cent between 1990 and 1995) and Zambia (where 95 per cent of

workers are still trapped below the $2-a-day poverty threshold).
Latin America fared little better, with the jobless total during
the 1990s soaring from 7.6 million to 18.1 million. In Brazil net
employment fell by 2.7 million during this decade, while farming
jobs in Mexico slumped from 8.1 million to 6 million between
1990 and 2006. An EU impact assessment of the completion
of the WTO Doha round found that 7.5 million jobs would be
at risk in Argentina, Brazil, Colombia, Costa Rica, Indonesia,
Mexico, the Philippines, Tunisia and Uruguay.

Contrary to neo-liberal propaganda, countries become
rich, not through free trade in the initial stages, but through
protectionism. Britain imposed ferocious tariffs on almost all
manufactured goods in the eighteenth century, and between 1864
and 1913 the US was the most heavily protected nation on earth,
and the fastest-growing. The UK and the US only discovered
their enthusiasm for free trade after they had achieved economic
dominance. The same strategy was followed by Germany, Japan,
South Korea, Taiwan and almost every other country that is rich
today. Protectionism, which can easily be exploited by corrupt
elites, does not guarantee the delivery of wealth; but development is much harder without it. By contrast free trade imposed
on poor countries in the early stages of their development
threatens to beggar them, as the EU 'economic partnership
agreements' (as they are euphemistically and misleadingly called)
would certainly do if inflicted on the African, Caribbean and
Pacific (ACP) nations, some seventy-six of the world's poorest
countries. The free-trade instruments deployed – removing trade
tariffs, making privatisation legally irreversible, prohibiting the
use of capital controls in a financial crisis – put developing countries at the mercy of wider international economic forces which

they are prevented from resisting, and would only benefit the multinational corporations of the rich world.

The fourth major downside in the international performance of neo-liberalism lies in the grotesque scale of accelerating inequality which this extreme form of capitalism has brought about across the world. At the end of the nineteenth century the income difference between the world's richest fifth and its poorest fifth has been variously estimated at between 3:1 and 6:1. By 1960 it was 30:1, and by 1997 it had reached a staggering 74:1. In 1998 the world's richest 1 per cent received the same income as the poorest 57 per cent. The speed of growth in inequality is unprecedented in human history and reflects the degree to which the neo-liberal economic model hugely disproportionately benefits the already rich and above all the already extremely rich. Moreover the huge leap in levels of global inequality has not altered the picture of persistent global poverty. Half the world's population is still forced to survive on less than $2 a day. This colossal stretch in hyper-inequality in both power and wealth is by any standards sustainable neither internationally nor domestically. Indeed, politically, the acrimonious collapse of the Hong Kong WTO negotiations in December 2005, the stranding of the so-called Doha development round ever since, the emergence of the blocking Group of Twenty leading developing countries at Cancun in 2006, and the increasing resistance to the Washington consensus, not least from China, strongly suggest the stirrings of a new world order.

(2) THE RISE OF THE DEVELOPING ECONOMIES

As a result of the huge and rapid rise of state-dominated capitalism, together with the Western financial–economic collapse in the decade from 2007, it is clear that a new world order is indeed fast coming into being. The combined output of the developing economies accounted for 38 per cent of world GDP at market exchange rates in 2010,[117] having doubled its share in just twenty years, and on this market exchange rate basis could well exceed the rich world's share by 2018. If, however, GDP is measured at purchasing power parity (i.e. lower prices in poorer countries boost real spending power), emerging economies have already overtaken the developed world by 2008 and reached 54 per cent of world GDP by 2011. Even more significantly, they accounted for three-quarters of global real GDP growth over the last decade, and now undertake over half of all world capital spending.

In other respects too the emerging world is edging ahead. In 2010 it accounted for over half of world exports, nearly double its share in 1990. In 2010 it also attracted more than half of total world FDI, luring foreign firms by its fast-growing domestic markets even more than by its lower wages. It now consumes 60 per cent of the world's energy (including 55 per cent of oil) and 75 per cent of all the world's steel. In 1995 emerging economies had only 5 per cent of the Fortune Global 500 firms; now, they have nearly a quarter. In terms of finance, their share of world stock market capitalisation is now 35 per cent, a tripling within a decade, and they hold no less than 81 per cent of governments' foreign exchange reserves while at the same time being responsible for only 17 per cent of all outstanding government debt. All of that augurs strongly for the future of the developing world, with enormous and still rapidly growing economic muscle, less

---

117   *The Economist*, 6 August 2011.

debt, more favourable demography and huge potential to raise productivity.

As economic power shifts decisively eastwards, how will that alter the shape of global institutions? The financial architecture under which first free market capitalism and more latterly state-dominated capitalism gained ascendancy over the past three decades was based primarily on the Bretton Woods settlement of 1944. It was erected around the liberalisation of capital movements, an open trading system and the deregulation of markets, with the uniform application of monetary policy across most of the world economy. It was designed to optimise the interests of the most powerful economies, notably the US, and to open up so far as feasible the rest of the world within a single market system which would maximally benefit the big Western corporations. Until the great crash of 2008 it largely achieved that purpose, though at high cost to the developing world, as outlined in Section 1 of this chapter. For that very reason, now that the tables are being turned, quite apart from theoretical economic analysis, that whole system will slowly but steadily give way to a very different framework.

(3) THE NEED FOR CAPITAL CONTROLS AND OTHER STABILISING MECHANISMS

Footloose capital assumes it is right and desirable to have an equalisation of interest rates in all parts of the world. However, Keynes managed to insert into the IMF Articles of Agreement the right of all member countries to 'exercise such controls as are necessary to regulate international capital movements', even though the untrammelled power of international capital over the last three decades reduced this largely to a dead letter. With that power now on the defensive, several proposals are now being made, not merely tactically (e.g. registration of financial dealers, greater disclosure of information, increased liquidity require-ments etc.), but aimed at a wholly different strategic objective and focused around one central component: capital controls, in particular the damping down of unstable movements of short-term capital ('hot money').

Malaysia did exactly this in introducing exchange controls in September 1998. These included measures to restrict interna-tional trade in their national currency and forcing immediate repatriation of their foreign-held national currency, a currency peg against the US dollar, the prohibition of secondary-market stock trading and of share sales by non-residents before one year of ownership, plus foreign exchange restrictions relating to trade, investment, domestic credit, and travel and educa-tion. Contrary to all the disasters predicted by neo-liberal proponents, the results were highly beneficial to Malaysia. Foreign investment in the country actually increased and amid the full-blown financial crisis suffered by the east Asian 'tigers' in that year, the downturn for Malaysia was much shal-lower.[118] The lesson of that episode is that whatever the pull of ideology and political prejudice, investors respond to political realities. Malaysia does indeed demonstrate that it is practicable for any one country to regain national control over its economy and to set its own monetary targets and policies, but of course what is really needed is the restoration of capital controls by international agreement.

Several other measures are necessary too. In order that actions to damp down flows of hot money do not inhibit a stable flow

---

118   Gould, B., *The End of Politics*, 2006, p. 100.

of long-term investment capital, Soros has proposed a new international institution be given responsibility to insure and guarantee international loans and guarantees up to specified limits. This is highly relevant given that the 2009 crash left developing countries with a funding gap of up to $700 billion a year as a result of inflows of foreign capital drying up. The new international machinery could be funded by a Tobin tax, originally proposed in 1972 to discourage speculation in currency markets while at the same time providing resources for genuine world development purposes. Even at the very low rate of 0.1 per cent the tax could still raise revenue of well over $200 billion a year.

Another problem of deregulated markets that needs reform is the instability of exchange rates under a floating-rate regime, especially since such markets regularly overshoot and respond irrationally in the face of incomplete information. Without returning to fixed rates, which produced their own problems in devaluation crises in the 1960s and 1970s, one solution might be a 'crawling peg' by which adjustments could be made at regular (e.g. monthly) intervals so that any intervening movements would be small and manageable. A variation of this would be to make intervention automatic rather than discretionary, carried out by a special stabilisation fund administered by an international group of central bank and other officials.[119] If that were not practicable on a global scale it could be set up on a regional basis, and indeed if the euro were finally to collapse on the grounds that a single currency was incompatible with competing with the German economy then a regular crawling peg operated

---

119   Grieve Smith, J., *Closing the Casino*, Fabian Society, 2000.

automatically in accordance with agreed criteria might provide an alternative mechanism for a resuscitated EU trading system, especially since it would offer a workable channel towards economic convergence.

Much will depend on the formation of a new political consensus. UNCTAD has shown that many of these approaches have actually been proved by countries which developed successfully in the past, such as Brazil, Japan and South Korea, all of which had publicly financed and managed development banks with a mandate to support the national economy. But the dominance of the Washington consensus and its demands for minimal state intervention, constant pressure to force down inflation at whatever cost to incomes and public services, and general market-led laissez-faire drove all such ideas to the margins for three decades. Now that that pressure is weakened, a more sensible balance can be drawn between inflation control and other key objectives of economic policy, especially full employment, an effective level of public services and a safer and more sustainable environment.

In addition, now that the Multilateral Agreement on Investment has been aborted, which aimed to guarantee the rights and privileges of international investors, notably the biggest Western corporations, against the interests of local populations, an international agreement in reverse should now be sought specifying the conditions under which investment might be acceptable in relation to the needs and interests of the indigenous population. And against the argument that any such experiment would rapidly lead to a boycott imposed by major investors, history has shown that that was not the experience of countries like Malaysia and China which took such a step.

(4) A REFORMED INTERNATIONAL FINANCIAL FRAMEWORK

As the emerging world steadily consolidates not only economic parity but also the political weight to influence the global consensus, many other equally profound changes will gradually refashion the international economy. Where global imbalances remain in trade and finance, though they should be much reduced by these reforms, a new Bretton Woods should establish, as Keynes rightly argued for in 1944, that the responsibility for restoring equilibrium should be jointly shared by creditor as well as debtor countries. The World Bank and IMF, if they survive at all alongside the new institutions proposed here, should no longer be dominated by the US and EU, but operate with a broader remit and under much more balanced control.

At present the World Bank operates on the principle of 'economically weighted' voting that gives over half the votes to just seven of the world's 190 countries, namely the G7. Despite its remit to deal with global poverty, it does not recognise any duty to respect and protect human rights, it repeatedly makes privatisation a condition for any aid, and it increasingly uses its private sector arm (the International Finance Corporation) to lend increasing amounts to corporate operations in middle-income countries. Half of the IFC's funding is now routed through hedge funds, private equity and other financial vehicles. The IMF is equally anti-democratic, giving the rich an inbuilt majority of votes to dominate the poor world. The US has a blocking minority against any constitutional change it disap-proves of, and the UK and France have more voting power than the forty-nine African members. Of even greater concern than its secrecy and arrogance is its poor record – derided for its fail-ure to predict most crises and then for its counter-productive responses, it is famed for congratulating bubble economies on their sound financial management just months before they spectacularly crashed, and blamed for rigid and uniform prescriptions that have made economic contractions much worse.

The World Bank and IMF remain the instruments by which Western financial markets project their power into the rest of the world. As such they are unacceptable to the alternative BRIC power axis as well as to the emerging economies, and will never properly perform the roles for which they were ostensibly set up. What is needed are very different institutions – a World Central Bank that can lend to countries under speculative attack, without the penalty of a conditional IMF bail-out, and a World Finance Authority with power to regulate the world's hedge funds and investment banks so as to make speculation more difficult and expensive. And the aura of globalisation as the goal of the international economy, in reality the basis for Western multinationals to dominate, needs to be replaced by regional groupings where that would better assist states in the early stages of development until they felt ready to participate in a fully open trading system.

CHAPTER XVIII

ENVIRONMENT: FROM UNCONTROLLED MARKETS TO GREEN ECONOMY

(I) THE ECOLOGICAL LIMITER

The fourth pillar of the edifice to create a Britain for the 99 per cent, not the elite, is – in addition to radical reconstruction of the economy (finance and manufacturing), society (breaking down inequality and class) and power structure (banks, big business, media and government) – a transformation of attitudes and policies towards the environment. Chapter III spelt out the combined pincer impact on the earth's carrying capacity of water and oil shortages, population over-reach, global warming and climate turmoil, and the finitude of resource availability in relation to the demands being made upon it. The importance of this fourth pillar as humanity slowly but steadily bumps up against the ecological limits can be gauged from a European study of ecosystems in 2008, which estimated the losses from the financial crash at $1–1.5 trillion (a total that has now risen by 2011–12 to some $2–3 trillion) while the loss of natural capital *from deforestation alone* was calculated at $2–5 trillion *every year*.[120] This total was reached by estimating the value of the services, such

---

120 Sukhdev, P., Deutsche Bank, European Report, 2008.

as locking up carbon and providing fresh water, which forests perform and then calculating the cost of either replacing them or living without them.

In one sense both crises have derived from the same cause. Those who have engaged in the exploitation, whether of financial artefacts or natural resources, have demanded unsustainable rates of return and invoked indebtedness that can never be repaid, while living in denial of the inevitable consequences of impending dislocation. This is a phenomenon that can be seen throughout history. There are many examples of ecological crisis becoming the catalyst to social catastrophe – e.g. Easter Island, the eleventh-century Zambezi kingdom in southern Zimbabwe, the Mayan civilisation in central America, to name but a few. The reasons why peoples fail to avert ecological collapse are strangely familiar. The resources at first appear inexhaustible. The long-term trend of depletion is fudged over by short-term fluctuations. A powerful elite consolidate their interests at the expense of everybody else. Assurances are given that technology and innovation will solve all problems.[121] Today's world is vastly more sophisticated, but the same hubris and the same nemesis apply. Cutting down the last tree on Easter Island has its parallel in draining the last, deepest oil-well five miles below the oceans, especially when by mid-century the global population whose wants must be serviced will be a million times greater than that of the Pacific island.

(2) BETWEEN A ROCK AND A HARD PLACE

But given the gargantuan pressures driving the capitalist expansion system and its controlling influence over current global

---

121 Monbiot, G., *Guardian*, 14 October 2008.

culture, is there any means of achieving a transition towards ultimate sustainability in human management of the earth? And can such a transition be effected before the exponential growth of exploitation brings about the cataclysmic dislocation and collapse that have regularly happened before in history, this time potentially on a much more catastrophic scale? At present, it has to be admitted, the evidence is pessimistic. Simply painting growth green – the fashionable idea behind so-called 'sustainable development' that economy, society and environment can be given equal weights – doesn't work: economic growth always turns out the dominant variable. Equally, the optimistic belief that clever technology can effectively decouple growth from environmental impacts is a mirage. Thus average global carbon intensity would have to be 130 times lower by mid-century to meet climate goals in an equitable world of steady population and economic growth, falling from 770 grams of CO_2 per dollar of output today to just 6 grams by 2050[122] – a scenario which will be greeted as utopian.

Nevertheless, there are signs of a different consciousness arising which, however seemingly insubstantial at first, may steadily erode the foundations of our ruthlessly exploitative civilisation. The fundamental issue is: what is growth *for*? NEF (the New Economics Foundation) has drawn attention to the range of international surveys showing that beyond an annual income level of some $15,000 per head, life satisfaction barely changes between countries with wholly different levels of GDP. There seems to be a definite level beyond which extra income does not deliver extra well-being.[123] Of course, the means of measurement

122 Jackson, T., *Prosperity without Growth: Economics for a Finite Planet*, Earthscan, 2009.
123 New Economics Foundation, (1) *The Great Transition*; (2) *Growth Isn't Possible*; (3) *21 Hours* (a call for a 21-hour working week).

is crucial here. GDP is unanimously promoted by the economic elite because its distributional impacts are strongly skewed to serve its own interests. But it is an inadequate measure of performance on several grounds. It does not distinguish between income and capital, thus paving the way for the liquidation of natural resources and a mountain of unsustainable credit to be treated as growth. It ignores the social dimension of economic activity, thus masking vast gulfs on inequality via per capita statistics. And it takes the market valuation of prices as a given, though both the financial crash and the growing awareness of the decoupling of wealth from happiness should make us deeply wary of this assumption.

If human well-being rather than GDP is the ultimate objective, what needs to be measured is the efficiency with which fundamental inputs into the economy, such as natural resources from an overstretched biosphere, are turned into desirable and meaningful human outcomes in the form of relatively long and satisfied lives. Standard, comparable international data now exist to supply these measures for most countries, and significantly they correspond quite closely with other quantitative data on, for example, health, depression and suicide. Combining these survey results on satisfaction with life expectancy produces some arresting conclusions. Despite all the fashionable praise for successful, knowledge-driven, resource-light service economies, the core European countries have in general become less carbon efficient at delivering well-being for their citizens than they were in 1961.[124]

However, both in Europe and particularly in the UK people

---

124   Simms, A., 'Moral Compass', *Resurgence*, November 2007.

report comparable levels of well-being whether their lifestyles are high-consuming and very resource intensive or low-consuming with a much smaller ecological footprint. If the former were deployed worldwide, it would imply the need for six and a half planets, while the latter might fit into the one planet we actually have. But it does imply that a lower level of consumption need not undermine quality of life and that governments' fear of demand management may be greatly overstated. The UK emerged twenty-first out of thirty countries analysed, with nations following the Anglo-Saxon economic model shown as the least efficient. Scandinavia, on the other hand, was the most efficient in achieving the highest levels of well-being in Europe at relatively low environmental cost.

The implications of this analysis are huge. It isn't just the relentless running down of natural capital (already at some 130 per cent of the reproduction rate of the planet) or the shortage of key resources like water and oil, nor even the constant growing threat of climate change. It is rather that the current dynamics of the international economy are producing diminishing returns for what should be the whole objective of the economic process – the maximising of human quality of life, well-being and happiness spread as equally as possible across the globe. Again, this is scarcely surprising. Billions of dollars and pounds are spent by marketing agencies, targeting children as young as two as well as their parents, to instil the belief that material possessions will ensure them the love and appreciation they crave. The global media now reaches into the most remote parts of the planet to spread the ubiquitous underlying message that 'to be seen, heard, appreciated and loved, you need the right trainers, jeans, toys and gadgets'. But such consumption breeds greater competition and envy, which makes children and young people feel more isolated, insecure and unfulfilled, thus unleashing even more frantic consumption in a vicious cycle. The global consumer culture taps into the universal human need for love, community and relationships and turns it into insatiable greed.[125]

Yet the task of confronting the human costs of growth has hardly begun. It certainly means challenging and dismantling the insidious culture of consumerism. It also means recognising that income inequality rather than the lack of particular levels of GDP are the cause of so much social pathology – loss of trust, mental ill-health, drug use, poor educational attainment, higher murder and violence rates, lower life expectancy, obesity etc.[126] And if endless growth is to be dethroned as the commanding goal of the industrialised world, a new ecological macroeconomics is needed which sets out a framework for scaling investments in resource efficiency, clean technologies and ecosystem enhancement. It will require a radical reconfiguration of the GDP of rich countries, which at present spend at least 15–20 per cent on human capital investments in health and education but just 1 per cent on the whole environmental foundation of people's well-being.[127]

(3) MODELS FOR ECONOMIC SUSTAINABILITY

How might such a vast transformation be achieved? One response is that it will be carried through by natural forces, however brutally or violently, because the indefinite continuation of present trends is impossible. In a world of nine billion

---

125 Norberg-Hodge, H., 'Economics of Happiness', *Resurgence*, November 2007.
126 Wilkinson, R., and Pickett, K., *The Spirit Level*, Allen Lane, 2009.
127 Robins, N., The Ecology of Growth, Resurgence, July 2010.

people, all aspiring to a level of income based on 2 per cent growth on the average EU income today, carbon intensities, for example, would have to fall on average by over 11 per cent a year to stabilise the climate, sixteen times faster than they have done since 1990 (the Kyoto Protocol base year). In reality there is as yet no credible, socially just, ecologically sustainable scenario of continually growing incomes for a world of nine billion people, and simplistic assumptions that capitalism's propensity for efficiency can find a way out are sheer fantasy, given the colossal and ever growing scale of the outcome required.

Nor is the conventional answer of 'decoupling' – that is, the idea that economic growth can continue with constantly declining material throughput – adequate as a response to this dilemma. Even *relative* decoupling has been declining globally since 2000 in some key structural materials such as iron ore, bauxite and cement; but far more worrying, *absolute* decoupling (i.e. overall reduction in resource throughput) is virtually absent. Such improvements in energy and carbon intensity as there have been over the last two decades have been swamped by the increase in the scale of economic activity over the same period (e.g. global carbon emissions from energy use have risen over this period by 40 per cent). Nor is even low-carbon industrialisation the obvious answer that many assume. The pioneering report *Climate Solutions 2* estimated that some twenty clean energy, energy efficiency, low-carbon agriculture and sustainable forestry sectors will need to grow by 20–24 per cent every year for the next four decades if greenhouse gas emissions are to be stabilised, yet only three of these sectors are on track.

The much more radical solution of a steady-state economy (SSE) has been proposed by the environmental economist

Herman Daly. He defines it as an economy with constant population and constant stock of capital, maintained by a low rate
of throughput that the ecosystem can assimilate and regenerate,
together with low production rates equal to low depreciation
rates. He envisages several mechanisms to implement this, in
particular a cap-auction-trade system for basic resources which
would limit the scale of resource extraction while allowing efficient allocation through trading. Ecological tax reform would
shift the tax base from value added (labour and capital) and on to
resources extracted from nature, put through the economy, and
returned back to nature (pollution). The remaining commons of
natural capital (e.g. rainforests and the atmosphere) would be
protected in public trusts and priced.

The national accounts would be reformed by separating GDP
into a cost account and a benefits account, with the implicit stricture
to stop growing when marginal costs equal marginal benefits. Wider
reforms would be consequential. International commerce would be
re-regulated to move away from unfettered free trade, free capital
mobility and globalisation. The present IMF–World Bank–WTO
framework would shift towards Keynes's plan for a multilateral
payments clearing union, charging penalty rates on surplus as well
as on deficit balances. The banking system would be moved towards
100 per cent reserve requirements instead of the present fractional
reserve banking, and control of the money supply would be put in
the hands of government rather than the private banks.

This transitional programme may seem radical, but it is still
based on the conservative institutions of private property and
decentralised market allocation. As Daly has himself acknowledged, these principles simply recognise that private property
loses its legitimacy if too unequally distributed, and that markets

lose their legitimacy if prices fail to tell the full truth about costs. The macroeconomy also becomes an absurdity if its scale is structurally required to grow beyond the biophysical capacities of the earth. Even before that physical limit the world is already encountering the conservative economic limit in which the extra costs of growth exceed the extra benefits.[128]

Some of these reforms have been advocated elsewhere in this book for other reasons, but the combination of all these measures in one all-encompassing package would require systematic cross-government analysis, both national and international, of all the wider implications and the methods and timing of their implementation. Sadly, it is unlikely that any transformation on such a scale would be seriously attempted until a catastrophe, or more likely a series of catastrophes, made it absolutely clear that continuing with business as usual was insupportable and that small modifications of existing practices would not cope either. Nevertheless Daly's SSE plan does provide a valuable outline of a possible blueprint for transition to a sustainable economy. He may well be right that if and when the world reaches this point, which is likely within the next century, small-scale adaptations won't work and there will be no alternative but either to continue as before and suffer continent-wide dislocation and a huge decline in the global population, or to 'flip' to a wholly different paradigm of interconnecting ecological parameters.

(4) THE POLITICS OF TRANSITION

To avoid this apocalypse, several studies have outlined detailed plans as to how a comprehensive environmental transition might

---

128   Daly, H., 'A Steady-State Economy', Sustainable Development Commission, July 2008.

be navigated consistent with commercial logic and involving minimum disruption. The ex-Treasury economist Nicholas Stern has set out systematically the reasons why high-carbon growth will eventually destroy itself as fossil fuel prices rise and the physical impacts of climate change start to bite widely and deeply.[129] The UN economist Lester Brown's Plan B proposes creating a new infrastructure and economy based on true-cost accounting, with honest markets and a five-fold increase in renewable energy, but embracing also extensive research on how to restore natural support systems, eradicate poverty, stabilise populations, rescue failing states and feed eight billion people.[130] Tim Jackson's 'Prosperity without Growth' questions whether growth is still a legitimate goal for rich countries, for reasons of human happiness as much as ecological necessity, and focuses as much on weakening the connection between rising incomes and well-being as on conforming to the environmental limits.

Yet these brave attempts at spelling out the full implications of major transition have so far been thwarted by a succession of political barriers. The all-encompassing intense rivalry between the US and China has undermined the 'green' momentum and stalled key international negotiations, most notably at Copenhagen in 2009. The enormous political muscle and lobbying power of the fossil fuel and nuclear industries, compared with a weak and fragmented renewables industry, has cowed governments into submission to their demands. The belief, sedulously propagated in much of the right-wing press, especially in the US, that an environmental transition would be risky and expensive

---

129   Stern, N., *A Blueprint for a Safer Planet*, Vintage, 2010.
130   Brown, L., *World on the Edge: How to Prevent Environmental and Economic Collapse*, Norton, 2011.

and would threaten today's comforts, has prevented the build-up of the critical mass of support in public opinion that would override the caution of political leaders.

But even in the short term the case for environmental transition remains compelling. The UK is better placed, because of its island location in the eastern Atlantic, to exploit wind power and wave and tidal power than any other EU country. Yet it generates only 5 per cent of its electricity from renewables, the lowest in the EU except for Malta and Luxembourg, well below the 10–25 per cent of France, Germany or Italy, and far below Scandinavia's 35–50 per cent. In wind turbine technology, where it might expect to be a world leader, the UK has been surpassed by Denmark and Germany. A study in 2008 found that Germany had created a renewable energy sector employing 249,000 with a turnover of €24 billion, yet the UK had only an estimated 7,000 jobs and a turnover of just €0.3 billion. In Spain the Building Technical Code made solar thermal energy resources compulsory in new and refurbished buildings, while in the UK the feed-in tariff rates were abruptly halved in 2012, thus flattening an emerging solar power industry, with 5,000 jobs lost and Chinese solar panels imported instead.

The UK has the best marine energy resource in Europe, with potential to supply 20 per cent of current electricity demand and create 10,000 jobs by the end of this decade, but then in 2011 the £50 million marine renewable deployment fund was closed down. The UK was keen to promote carbon capture and storage technology, but has allowed Canada and Australia and twenty other demonstration projects to get under way first while it continues to dither. The Tory government initially decided to abandon a third runway at Heathrow in favour of a new high-speed rail link to the north, but then after heavy industrial lobbying is minded in 2013 to go ahead with a huge extension in flights (and the consequential carbon emissions) from Heathrow. Even the Green Deal, claimed to create 100,000 insulation jobs by 2015 and reach twenty-four million homes by 2020, is now expected to reach only a fifth of that number of households, while fuel poverty climbs to afflict nine million by 2016.

Clearly, the economic and logistical problems of achieving a transition to a low carbon, energy efficient, 'green' transformation of the international economy are immense. But the fundamental problem at this stage remains that the politics, both domestic and international, are still moving in the opposite direction. Despite some advances that are hesitant and fragmentary, Britain is still held in thrall to an outdated 'ancien régime' incapable of reforming itself, yet dragging the country ever deeper into unsustainability.

CHAPTER XIX

AN UNFINISHED AGENDA

(I) PROBLEMS NOT YET ADDRESSED

Britain is still only at the very early stages of a fundamental transformation. The neo-liberal capitalist system which has dominated the world for the last three decades is finished, though its proponents and apologists refuse to recognise the fact, but it was irreversibly broken by the Great Financial Crash of 2008–9 and the ensuing global depression, and is anyway rejected by the fast-emerging and soon-to-be-dominant economies of east Asia and parts of the Southern world. However, there is no consensus about a replacement; indeed, there is a distinctly arid ideological landscape. The world remains for the moment in that painful state where the past hegemony is now dead but a new one is not yet born.

For Britain itself this underlying problem of the ideological vacuum is further complicated by its being bound up with the country's own specific dilemma, namely that its economic, social and environmental policies are unsustainable and rapidly approaching impasse. What is needed is an uncompromising positive vision of the fundamental changes required to restore Britain to a sustainable and successful course in its industry and finance, in the integrity of its society, in its environmental

approach, its values and culture, and indeed its power structure.
This whole book is intended as a contribution precisely to that
end. Yet there are still central questions for that vision which
remain unresolved, and are scarcely even being addressed. Some
of the more important ones are discussed in the rest of this
section, though there are many more.

One question that was raised but not answered in Chapter
XVI is: under a system aimed to run capitalism in the national
interest rather than that of shareholders and investors, how is
accountability to be restored when those shareholders and investors have clearly lost control? That is only likely to be resolved,
not at the level of capital alone, but rather by a new settlement
between managers and their workforce. A new framework of
control, similar to the German *Mitbestimmung* (co-determina-
tion) model imposed, ironically enough, by the Allies after the
war, would provide equal voting rights between management and
employee representatives on a board carrying oversight of the
whole enterprise, while leaving senior management with day-
to-day executive responsibility. The workforce representatives
would need their own independent advisers, whether accountants, lawyers or trade union experts, so that they could engage
fully on an equal basis with the management team.

The underlying basis of this arrangement would be that the
workforce and their advisers would be kept informed and fully
consulted before any major decisions were taken, and their views
fully taken into account, while the workforce and the trade
unions on their side would undertake to forgo the strike weapon
except as a last resort in extreme situations. That would have the
advantage of providing the trade unions with a much more positive role in industrial relations, as well as significantly reducing

disruption and offering the employees a much stronger sense of participation in the enterprise. This sense of identification with and commitment to the organisation would be strengthened further still if the proposals were adopted, as set out in Chapter XIII, for remuneration from boardroom to shop floor to be determined via whole-company pay bargaining.

A second, wider question is: how can the key strategic standards and objectives of public policy be met in an economy when almost all industries and services have been privatised, at least until such time as some of these privatisations are reversed? When many key public services are now being performed in the private sector, this could be secured by regular NAO audits of the top five companies in the main economic sectors, scrutinising performance in terms of employment conditions, utilisation of (scarce) natural resources, energy efficiency, greenhouse gas emissions, waste generation, water use and pollution. This would emphasise that the object of economic activity is not simply the maximisation of returns to capital by whatever means, but rather that competitiveness is secured consistent with the achievement of other essential public objectives. This reconciliation of public and private goals is consistent both with the German *Mittelstand* concept of relational banking and partnership with stakeholders and with MITI-style harmonisation of public policy objectives with industrial efficiency, both of which in their time were key aspects of highly successful economies.

Another central question, much discussed but very little followed through in practice in any meaningful way, is the whole issue of citizen empowerment within a capitalism designed not to maximise the wealth of a controlling elite but to optimise the national interest of all its people. There are several ideas here that need to be tested and developed. The study of Britain's social, economic and political systems could be made a compulsory subject within the curriculum in education so that people would be better able to understand the ways in which power works, get more involved, obtain redress and assert their rights. It would enormously expand horizons in terms of opportunities and self-confident navigation of an increasingly complex, closed and stratified society.

A more knowledgeable public could result in demands that the press offer more factual and objective accounts of events, so that people would be much better informed about the real state of the country instead of settling for the pap delivered daily in the tabloids. The public could be given effective powers of accountability or recall against MPs, ministers and police in the public sector as well as, via the intermediate operation of the political system, against banks, corporations, media and any other repositories of power that afflict their lives. And NGOs could be empowered to take companies to court, paid by public funds, where there was a public interest justification in doing so and where it could be shown prima facie that the organisation had breached mandatory environmental, social or labour standards.

Another empowering role is to find new imaginative ways to make democracy more effective. At present, democracy is not seen by political leaders as a shared partnership with the electorate in the exercise of power, but rather as an inconvenience which by spin, manipulation and selective news management can be gradually eroded or even turned to partisan advantage. Britain is currently not so much a democracy at all as an oligarchy run by the banks, corporations, media and No. 10, or perhaps even more accurately a market plutocracy. Certainly a vote every four to five years does not constitute a real democracy, and the ancient distractions (Juvenal's contemptuous reference 2,000 years ago to *'panem et circenses'*) are still regularly deployed in modern form (sport, TV and celebrity gossip) sufficiently to lull the body politic into comatose acquiescence. A vibrant democracy demands much more effective instruments to gain traction for the public on their rulers. Such additional channels of influence could include referenda on key issues according to predetermined criteria, electronic access for citizens during the scrutiny of bills in Parliament, a right to have issues of national importance that have attracted a high threshold of signatures to be debated and voted on in the House, and a new select committee appointed to tour the country on a regular basis to receive and discuss public petitions and refer them as appropriate to ministers or other select committees. And enabling councils to retain greater control over their own tax resources, and devolving the allocation of a significant proportion of this (perhaps 5 per cent) to local consultation and democratic choice of the local electorate, would for the first time seriously empower local communities.

The same empowerment could be pursued through new formations within the economy. A sense of proprietary control, both in terms of rights and responsibilities, would be conveyed through the encouragement of co-operatives, mutuals and employee ownership schemes, which could be promoted by a mixture of grants and tax reliefs. The development of enterprise councils could bring about much more systematic sharing of information with employees across the company. Existing highly successful experiments, for example in co-ownership, could be greatly extended. These already account for £20 billion turnover (1.5 per cent of the UK economy), covering such diverse sectors as retail (John Lewis), civil engineering (Arup) and advertising (St. Luke's), and have been found to produce a 19 per cent productivity uplift in a more engaged employee environment.[131] And some new constructions could take novel forms, like the Norwegian state pension funds, which were made a beneficiary of the country's oil revenues and are now worth some £230 billion. Yet another example are the Swedish Meidner wage-earner funds which received a regular share levy (around 10 per cent of profits), which over time promoted a new regime of corporate governance.

Then there are the big international questions that still need answering. How are the colossal conglomerations of private economic power, represented by hedge funds (whose assets increased from $39 billion in 1990 to $1.7 trillion in 2007), private equity and sovereign wealth funds contracted to private fund managers, to be held to account? How do we ensure optimal utilisation of limited resources to secure long-term growth, full employment, a fair and proportionate distribution of income, and the infrastructure and services that emerging economies need for balanced global development? How can such funding flows be rechannelled to promote wider public objectives within the real economy? It will require detailed regulation of their activities, including *inter alia* quarterly presentation of their accounts, enumeration on a country-by-country basis of their funding spread, statement of sums deposited in each tax jurisdiction and tax paid, and the disposition of their investments to meet the mandatory requirement that a given proportion (say, at least 60 per cent) is directed towards approved areas of the

131   Reeves, R., *New Statesman*, 19 February 2007.

productive economy. Clearly it would be preferable for these rules to be established by international treaty, but even in the absence of such a treaty the UK should enforce them within its own jurisdiction.

How can an adequate level of aggregate demand be maintained for developing countries as their economies contract as a result of capital flight during the decade-long 2010s recession brought on by the follies of Western banking? There are a number of measures here that could substantially ease the problem. Access to special drawing rights by less developed countries (LDCs) could be significantly widened. The payment of (higher) minimum wages payable by multinational investors in LDCs could be enforced in the UK and the West. Less restrictive trade rules for LDCs (e.g. allowing primary producers to process and distribute their own commodities) could be introduced. The shameful structural adjustment programmes imposed by the IMF, which effectively recolonise LDCs for Western capital, should be abandoned. And the World Bank or its replacement should concentrate its £35 billion-a-year funding on relieving world poverty rather than providing market opportunities for private capital.

Another fundamental though not utopian issue, which again is much discussed though little acted upon, concerns the unpacking of the concepts of growth and value. At present, growth is measured by GDP, which bizarrely includes all economic activity as though it were of positive value (e.g. a train crash generating £100 million in track repairs is reckoned equal to uninterrupted service which generates £100 million in ticket sales). No deduction is made for the depreciation of natural capital (i.e. the overuse or degradation of soil, water, forests, fisheries and the atmosphere). There is no offset to take account of indebtedness.

A more refined 'measure of domestic progress' (MDP) is needed which will more accurately track the real advances and declines in human welfare. It should incorporate broad measures of inequality, crime levels, tax avoidance/evasion, social breakdown, environmental decay and climate change impacts, and national policies should then be focused much more sharply on countering these drawbacks to human well-being.

In addition, one important consequence of this assessment of wider social impacts could be a re-evaluation of the relative worth of different occupations. On the basis of contribution to the well-being of the nation, the New Economics Foundation in a seminal study in 2009 found that City workers, advertising executives and tax advisers actually destroyed value, while hospital cleaners, childcare workers and staff in the waste recycling industry gave much more to the country than they took out. The fact that high pay is often generated by businesses that destroy other parts of the economy (e.g. the value destruction caused by a banking crash or the overconsumption generated by advertising agencies) or fail to pay the full cost of their activities (e.g. tax avoidance facilitated by accountants and tax advisers) should be taken into account in training and recruitment patterns, in pay guidelines set down by a High Pay Commission and in eligibility for public contracts.

One last issue here (though there are of course many others) concerns the ideological battleground which will have to be fiercely fought over if real change is to happen. The ideal of the entrepreneurial, hyper-efficient private sector remains deeply embedded in contemporary Western culture, despite all the evidence against it. Even the right-wing American economist DeAnne Julius, commissioned by the UK government in

2008 to review the performance of the public service industry (sic) – responsible for 30 per cent of all healthcare, some
social care services and prisons, as well as consultancy, cleaning, IT etc. – concluded that the latest evidence showed that
the private sector did not have innate efficiency advantages.[132]
Other recent government studies have also found poorer private
sector performance. A DWP report in 2006 on Action Teams
for Jobs[133] showed private sector teams met only 78 per cent of
their job entry targets, while Jobcentre Plus (public sector) teams
exceeded theirs by 40 per cent.

An independent survey of this and other recent evidence[134]
concluded that 'it is simply not true that either the private or the
third sector has a consistently better record ... than in-house staff.
Wherever Jobcentre Plus has been allowed the same flexibilities
and funding ... it has been able to match, if not surpass, the
performance of contractors'. Nevertheless the relentless propaganda of private capital, so anxious to win lucrative contracts
in the public services, has been very successful in painting the
public sector as inherently inefficient and this constant impugn-
ing of the state, denigration of its capacity and dismissal of its
role have to be strenuously contested, not only as false and fabri-
cated for ulterior motives, but also as seriously detrimental to the
national interest.

But the intellectual rebirth of radicalism will only succeed if it
harnesses the array of social forces that are the ineluctable driver of
fundamental change. The ideology of national interest capitalism

---

132 Julius, D., PSI Review, 10 July 2008, http://www.bis.gov.uk/files/file46965.pdf
133 DWP, Action Teams for Jobs, 2006, http://research/dwp.gov.uk/asd/asd5/reports2005-6/
     rrep328.pdf
134 Davies, S., 'Contracting Out Employment Services to the Third and Private Sectors',
     Critical Social Policy, vol. 28, 2008.

set out here provides a coherent and detailed vision around which those forces might group as the first step in the replacement of the market fundamentalism model. Its measures press at the limits of capitalism, but will certainly be regarded as falling short of socialism. Nevertheless, ideologies evolve under pressure from the broad sweep of events and the gathering momentum of human aspiration. The belief that, while the market has its proper place, the fundamental principles underpinning society should be equity, social justice, equality of opportunity and democratic accountability is a rallying call that evokes a universal response. It is a fundamental change of direction which once launched knows no bounds.

INDEX